LITTLE SIR NICHOLAS

LITTLE
SIR NICHOLAS

❧

David Benedictus

❧

Based on a novel by C. A. Jones

BBC BOOKS

❦

Published by BBC Books,
a division of BBC Enterprises Limited,
Woodlands, 80 Wood Lane, London W12 0TT
First published 1990
© David Benedictus 1990
ISBN 0 563 20869 4

Set in Garamond by Ace Filmsetting Ltd, Frome, Somerset
Text and cover printed and bound in Great Britain by Richard Clay Ltd,
Bungay, Suffolk

◦◦

To Walter, Wally and Gerald in particular
and to the Writers' Guild of Great Britain
in general. With thanks.

◦◦

Chapter One

When the *SS Alberta* left harbour, there was a brisk breeze blowing and a light swell running. Perfect weather for sailing. There was no reason to suppose that the Channel crossing would be any different from a hundred others. Even when the wind veered round to a south-westerly and strengthened to a full gale, Captain Walter Tremaine continued to smile and sing snatches of old sea shanties to his beloved wife, Elizabeth, and Nicholas, his son.

Nicholas sat on a large wooden trunk which had his father's name in bold black letters upon it. He was as proud of it as it was possible to be proud of anything. In it, beautifully folded between layers of crinkly paper, lay all his worldly possessions, his books, his toys, and his clothes, notably the sailor suits which he wore on special occasions. He would be wearing them tomorrow at Trecastle House for his grandmama and grandpapa. And he felt sure that he would be wearing them for William Randle, his tutor.

Although Nicholas Tremaine was only four he had spent so much of his short life at sea that he considered it perfectly natural for his world to toss and turn, to pitch and roll, to creak and shudder. Ashore he became fretful and left his food on the plate. At sea he was as much a part of the universe as the sea-gulls and the flying fish.

His father, Captain Walter Tremaine, was unlike other sea captains who boasted about the imaginary wives they had in every port and seemed almost ashamed when they received letters from the real wives they had left at home. Walter Tremaine was so deeply in love with his wife that he could scarcely bear to be parted from her. So Nicholas slept in a tiny hammock, drank a daily sip of his father's grog and loved nothing better than to watch the porpoises dancing around the ship's prow and the flying fish leaping around her stern. And Elizabeth charmed the sailors, who had been brought up to believe that it was unlucky to have a woman on board ship, but could not imagine that a woman as beautiful and gentle as Elizabeth Tremaine could bring anything but good fortune to those around her.

Thunder had been rumbling around the *Alberta* for some time and crackles of lightning pierced the black clouds. Nicholas laughed to see them. Suddenly a massive wave struck the *Alberta* amidships and three of the seamen were sent sprawling. Elizabeth reached out for her son and clasped him tightly to her. As he was crushed against the shawl tied around her shoulders, Nicholas could smell the distinctive scent of violets which he always associated with his mother. He had never felt safer and dared the sea to do its worst.

The next wave was dark green. It rose like a huge hedge

in front of the ship, and kept on growing until it blotted out the sky and hovered above the main top sail, white blossoming at its crest. When it broke over the *Alberta*, it was as though a house had fallen on the deck. Billy, a young signalman, was up the mast and trying to furl the sail when lightning struck, and Billy was flung into the sea. Nobody saw him go and nobody heard him cry out, but when Walter shouted for a distress rocket, Billy was nowhere to be found. Already the helmsman had lashed himself to the wheel, and when the next mountain of water rose up before them, he turned the ship's prow with its proud figurehead into the wave. The thunder was continuous now; everywhere was fire and water and to the commotion was added the eerie shriek of the wind.

Now a whole range of waves was towering above the *Alberta*, and the helmsman braced himself, stiffening his legs and clasping the wheel, eyes shut and lips moving in a silent prayer. As the mountains of water struck the ship Elizabeth and Nicholas were sent sprawling across the deck. Captain Tremaine spied a coil of heavy rope attached to the mast and hurled himself at it, then thrust the loose end in his wife's direction. Elizabeth grabbed the rope and tied it around the boy's waist while Captain Tremaine attached the other end to a life-buoy. A group of sailors were fighting their way inch by perilous inch towards the life-boat, secured at the stern, but even as they reached it a pillar of water descended upon them and the life-boat was torn from its moorings. For a moment or two they watched in horror as it bobbed away across the foaming sea, but then a bolt of lightning struck it. It was sent spinning into the air, and by the time it fell back into the sea it was no more than spars and struts, just so much driftwood.

'I love you, Nico,' Elizabeth cried. 'Always remember that I love you.'

The boy could see her lips moving, and understood, but no human voice could make itself heard above the cacophony of the storm. A whining gust of wind snapped the main mast in two with a crack like the crack of a whip. The rigging crashed to the deck, pinning Captain Tremaine under a shroud of wet sail-cloth. Although badly hurt, he was still conscious and he stretched out his arms to his wife and son, only to see Elizabeth washed over the side. Attached to the life-belt and clinging grimly to the cords at the side of the trunk, Nicholas stayed on the deck for a minute or two longer. He saw his father and reached out his arms; but it was in vain. Another wave thrust trunk, boy and life-belt into the sea.

The water was a mass of driftwood and rigging. Nico could hear men cursing and praying, and then he sank below the surface. When he resurfaced he found himself near his beloved trunk which was bobbing in the foam. As he clambered on to the life-belt he suddenly found himself no more than a few yards from his mother. Her lustrous mass of auburn hair had escaped from its pins and was trailing around her in the water. She smiled at him; then, as though surrendering to the sea, ceased to struggle and sank gently from sight. He was never to see her again, except in his dreams. In his dreams he saw her almost every night; she never aged, she never struggled, she never stopped smiling. She smiled at him, and her hair swirled about her, and then she sank below the surface.

In the weeks and months and years that followed there were times when he wondered whether it had not all been a dream. The SS *Alberta*, his father, the Captain, the lightning and the wind and the waves, the sailors praying and

10

cursing, the split mast, the trunk, the foam, his mother drowning. When people asked him about his mother and father, he said he remembered nothing. It would have been more of a betrayal, he felt, if he had spoken of what he had seen, or what he thought he had seen, or what he dreamed he had seen. They were his own memories and belonged to no one else.

All that he had seen and known before that fateful trip on the *Alberta* – the large white house on the cliff, the starched maidservants, the rooms full of shelves of books from floor to ceiling, the sense of belonging, of being loved and honoured, the large soft bed and the silly toys – was as though it had never been.

Those still living there waited in vain for the return of the gallant Captain and his beautiful wife, and the young Sir Nicholas, upon whom all their hopes depended.

Chapter Two

In the years of which I write, Trecastle village in the county of Cornwall had a population of no more than five hundred souls. There was a natural harbour in which a dozen fishing boats bobbed cheerfully, and a steep path up to the village. There was a green with a duck pond, and a gaggle of bad-tempered geese. There was a general stores in which you could buy lemon sherbet and boot black, weevilly rice and mouse-traps, chalks and china cups and cheese. There was an old church built partly of wood and partly of flint, and an old vicar, the Reverend Clowes. His great passion was for bell-ringing and he had a fine peal of bells in the belfry. Unfortunately for the Reverend Clowes, it took him so long to heave himself up the steps to the belfry that his gallant team of bell-ringers frequently grew impatient, and had often decamped to the *Dun Cow* for a few pints of scrumpy and a game of skittles by the time the vicar appeared.

The school was just two rooms, one in which the children could learn everything the Misses Lappin could teach them, and one in which the Misses Lappin could fan their faces and blow their noses and quarrel. Miss Emilia Lappin did not approve of the way Miss Augusta Lappin encouraged the children to think for themselves, and Miss Augusta Lappin did not approve of the way Miss Emilia Lappin encouraged the children to laugh at Miss Augusta Lappin. Miss Emilia Lappin had a wooden leg, and when she got especially angry, Miss Augusta Lappin would kick it, throwing Miss Emilia Lappin off balance and startling her. It was an excellent school in which to study human nature, and the twenty children who attended it were as happy as they deserved to be, which for most of them was very happy indeed. There was also a cobbler's shop, and a draper's, and an ironmonger's, and a blacksmith.

Beyond the village was the Dower House, built of pink bricks with pink roses clinging to them and house martins nesting under the eaves. It was a handsome square house built in the reign of Queen Anne, and when the Misses Lappin asked the children to draw houses they usually drew houses very much like the Dower House. It was the home of Captain Walter Tremaine, his auburn-haired wife Elizabeth, and their son Nicholas, which meant that, except for servants, it was uninhabited for much of the year.

Up on the cliffs stood Trecastle House, the ancient seat of the Tremaine family, and the finest house for many miles around. Some said it was the finest in Cornwall. Around it grew clumps of rhododendron bushes, and fuchsias. There was a paddock with the prettiest of ponies, called Peterkin. Climbing up the walls of the stables was an apricot tree; once in the summer of 1822, Robinson, the old butler, insisted, it had been heavy with apricots, but Robinson had been a young man then and was now eighty.

There was no one to argue with him, because none of the staff had been alive in 1822, and Sir Nicholas had been sailing the seven seas with the East India Company, taking Bibles in the hold and returning with coffee and tea and cinnamon from Ceylon. One year, on All Fools' Day, two of the footmen had hung oranges on the apricot tree. Robinson had not been amused.

The season being summer, the weather fine and the air astir with butterflies, Trecastle House looked particularly cheerful. Robinson – it was impossible to think of him having any name other than Robinson – was supervising the erection of a triumphal arch bearing the words:

WELCOME HOME CAPTAIN WALTER

Sir Nicholas Tremaine, the old baronet and Captain Walter's father, was watching from the terrace and offering bad advice, which Robinson ignored. Finally the baronet removed a gold half-hunter watch from his waistcoat pocket, snapped it open and grunted. He was not good at waiting; being the most important man for miles around he had little practice at it. Lady Tremaine, dressed in magnificent purple silk, joined him.

'Robinson has posted Joe Snell and Tom Austen on the Truro road,' she said. 'Just as soon as they spy the dust from the carriage they will gallop to the church and the bells will be rung.'

William Randle trotted up carrying his easel. A school friend of Captain Walter, he had taken up painting and had been given the use of an empty house on the estate in return for tutoring young Nicholas. In the boy's absence, William was busily engaged on a series of watercolour paintings of Trecastle House, a generous commission from

15

Lady Tremaine, who had always had a weakness for a handsome face. He asked whether there was any news, but the Captain and his family were not expected to arrive until three.

'How is the painting progressing?' Lady Tremaine asked.

'It's coming along,' replied William.

'Do not forget to include the peacocks,' reminded Sir Nicholas.

'Indeed, they are there already, making a grand splash of colour.'

'Not too vulgar, I trust?'

'Can nature be vulgar?' William replied.

At which his employer grunted, for, when he was stumped for an answer, he usually found that a grunt served pretty well. It does when you are a baronet.

Time passed. Cobwebby clouds crossed the sun. The triumphal arch was erected.

Out on the Truro road two boys, Joe Snell and Tom Austen, were growing bored of waiting. They had tried rolling marbles, and they had tried whittling sticks, and they had tried crushing ants, but staring into the sun looking for a non-existent carriage seemed a pointless way of wasting an afternoon.

In the belfry of St Stephen's Church, the bell-ringers were also becoming fidgety. One of them, Joe Trewarthen, took out his clay pipe, but caught the eye of Tom Carter, who was in charge of the bell-ringing, and put it away again. In the vestry the Reverend Clowes thought about climbing up and giving a brief address on the virtue of patience, but the thought of all those steps – seventy-four, he had counted them many times – discouraged him, so he didn't.

Time passed. Clouds like linen sheets passed across the sun. Sea-gulls soared in the sky with mournful cries.

Lady Tremaine instructed Robinson to prepare some tea. She was growing cold, she said, and would wait indoors.

'Aye, Madam,' said her husband, 'you do that.'

'And you?'

'I stay.'

Randle proposed taking the carriage to Penzance. He explained that if he failed to meet them on the road he would discover the reason for the delay. He could also relieve Joe Snell and Tom Austen.

'It is good of you, William,' said Lady Tremaine.

'I shall be back by noon tomorrow. Sooner if I meet them on the road. You are not to fret.'

Lady Tremaine looked at him quizzically. 'Not fret? Not fret? Our son, his wife, our grandson? Certainly we shall fret.'

The boys were relieved from their post. The bell-ringers, disgruntled and tired of waiting, came down the steps from the belfry. Robinson served tea.

Not until the clouds that covered the sun were as thick as pillowcases, and a sea-mist came blowing in from the Atlantic, coating everything in a chilling moisture, did Sir Nicholas leave his post and walk indoors. His legs were stiff and he seemed to have aged ten years in the course of one afternoon.

*   *   *

It was the following day. The rain was cold and spiteful and the triumphal arch was looking very sorry for itself as William Randle drove the carriage through it. He reined in the horses directly in front of the stone portico. From the window of the library Sir Nicholas let out a sigh.

'He's back,' he said. 'He is alone.'

'Bear up, my dear,' said his wife, who had been turning the pages of an unread book. 'Whatever the news we shall face it together.'

There was a knock at the door. Robinson heaved his old frame into the room and stood aside as William, with a day's growth of stubble, entered.

'Well?'

'Nothing is certain, but reports have reached Penzance that the steam and sail packet *SS Alberta* foundered in heavy seas some distance off the Breton coast. No one has seen her since she left Cherbourg. No survivors have been picked up. What *is* known is that Captain Walter, Elizabeth and Nicholas Tremaine were on board when she set sail for Penzance.'

As he delivered this speech, which he had rehearsed many times over during the exhausting carriage drive, William knew that what he was telling them would break their hearts. He knew it, but he told them.

Lady Tremaine, who had got to her feet when he started to speak, now stood as though turned to stone. The rain on the gravel and the flapping of the triumphal arch formed a gloomy accompaniment to the scene. Sir Nicholas showed no sign of emotion as he turned to the young man.

'We are grateful to you, Randle. We would have been more grateful had the news been better.'

A bell tolling from the belfry of St Stephen's made itself heard. Lady Tremaine sat back in her chair and took a lace handkerchief from her cuff.

'So soon,' she whispered.

Chapter Three

Five years passed. Every Sunday the Reverend Clowes led his tiny congregation in prayers for the souls of Captain Walter, Elizabeth and Nicholas. In the front pew, reserved for the Tremaine family, Sir Nicholas and Lady Tremaine were the focus of all eyes. Sir Nicholas had suffered a stroke and walked with a stick. He spoke seldom but when he did speak the words came out strangely. Lady Tremaine wore black dresses which rustled when she moved. She had taken to spiritualism and, in the evenings after Sir Nicholas had made his painful way to bed, she was visited by mad-looking women who claimed to be in touch with the missing Tremaines. The servants reported hearing moanings and knockings when these sessions were in progress, and seeing flickering lights through chinks in the door, but whether or not Lady Tremaine received messages from the dead, the mad-looking women came less and less frequently to Trecastle House, and eventually stopped coming at all.

On the fifth anniversary of the tragedy a memorial service was held, and afterwards the elderly couple stood on the cliffs staring out to sea, the sea-gulls wheeling around their heads in sympathy. The following day Sir Nicholas retired to bed and stayed there.

A year later he died.

The day after his funeral Lady Tremaine appeared in a pale green dress and asked Robinson to join her in the morning room.

'Robinson,' she said, 'there has been enough mourning in this house. We have work to do. I wish you to post this letter. It is to Apted.'

Mr Apted was the family solicitor and lived in Lincoln's Inn, London. He knew everything there was to know about the law, and anything he did not know he made up. Since he was held in very high regard it really didn't matter.

At home, though, his wife and children believed nothing he said. They played practical jokes on him, and sewed the bottoms of his trousers together. The more he was bullied at home, the more pompous he became in his chambers in Lincoln's Inn. He looked a little like a ferret.

A few days after receiving Lady Tremaine's letter he presented himself at Trecastle House. He carried with him a Gladstone bag which appeared to be extremely heavy. Robinson showed him into the library and waited by the door. Lady Tremaine was sitting with the large family Bible in front of her. It was open at the family tree.

'Mr Apted,' she said, having promised him tea and a sponge cake when their business was concluded, 'now that my husband is dead, we have important business to attend to.'

'Concerning an heir to Trecastle?'

'Precisely. My late husband refused to accept that we were without an heir, but now we must find one. We must find one so that when I have passed on . . .'

With some difficulty Apted lifted his bag onto the table and removed from it two huge volumes, *Burke's Peerage* and *Principal Families of Cornwall*.

A little smugly he said: 'I guessed as much, and came prepared. It appears' – he unfolded a pair of gold-rimmed pince-nez and placed them on his nose – 'that there was a cousin of your late husband, a certain Joseph Tremaine . . .'

Robinson cleared his throat. 'If you will permit me, milady?'

'Well?'

'When I was a hall-boy here just after the Battle of Trafalgar we received a visit from a Joseph Tremaine, a rather noisy gentleman.'

'I never heard Sir Nicholas speak of him.'

'He was not much spoken of in the family, milady.'

Apted looked up from *Principal Families*. 'He married twice, and died leaving issue. Two children, it seems. A girl who died in infancy and a son, Edward, who worked for a time as a clerk in a London bank.'

'Trade!' muttered Lady Tremaine in a shocked voice.

'He is believed to have married, though to whom is not stated.'

'And where is he now?'

'Dead, Lady Tremaine, dead.'

Lady Tremaine looked much as though a Tremaine who worked as a bank clerk deserved no better fate.

'If Edward married it is probable that he had children. If there is a wife surviving, she would inherit; if a son, he would.'

'Pray God there be a son.'

'I propose that we place an advertisement in the London newspapers.'

'Excellent. An heir must be found.'

So when the tea had been drunk and the sponge cake consumed (Apted had a secret weakness for sponge cake), the family solicitor took his leave.

That evening as Lady Tremaine climbed the stairs to bed she lingered rather longer than usual before the William Randle portrait of her lamented grandson. There was young Nicholas in a sailor suit and a cocked hat and he was smiling so cheerfully that it seemed most probable that in the morning the old house would ring once more to his laughter. Lady Tremaine sighed deeply. Four candles had burned brightly in her heart and all had been snuffed out. But she had no more tears to shed.

Within a week advertisements had been lodged in all the London newspapers.

Chapter Four

Old Nolan said the strangest things, and you thought nothing of them at the time. It was only later that you realised that he had not quite said what you thought he had said.

'One of the strangest things about this shop,' Margaret had heard him say once to an elderly customer, 'is that the walls come *right down* to the floor.' The old gentleman who had only come in to have a pair of old boots resoled had not looked in the least surprised. Maybe he was a trifle deaf, but Margaret, waiting to be served, was bewildered. At the time she was just a little thing, no more than eight, and she had glanced furtively at the walls and where they joined the floor, and yes, they did join it all the way down and all the way round. For the next few months she had glanced at walls and floors in other rooms and had never yet seen a room in which the walls and floors did not meet. Years later she had said to Old Nolan:

'Do the walls still come right down to the floor?'

And without a moment's hesitation, as though this conversation was following straight on from the previous one, he had said:

'No, Margaret, not any more.'

Old Nolan's shop was to be found in a bleak and impoverished street in one of the poorest parts of the great city of London. Between Old Nolan's shop and St Paul's was a part of the city in which fortunes were made and lost – but more often made than lost – by the hour. The Royal Mint had vaults crammed with gold which it turned into golden sovereigns and half-sovereigns. Old Nolan's street was lucky if it saw a half-sovereign in a year, and the only place where you could conceivably expect to find one was in Statham's, the Pawnbrokers. The Bank of England issued bank notes and letters of credit and drafts and other mysterious documents which enabled those who possessed them to live like emperors merely by showing them. In Old Nolan's street the only notes issued were pawn-tickets and IOUs, and these tended to grow dog-eared and dirty long before they could be redeemed.

Nonetheless Things Happened in Old Nolan's shop. It was never a simple matter of bringing in a pair of boots, explaining what needed doing to them, and leaving. More was required of you than that. You might be expected to hold forth on philosophy, or turn a cart-wheel, or recite a poem by Tennyson, and, if you did so, you might be given a discount on your boots. On the other hand, if Old Nolan did not care for your face or your conversation he might very well charge you extra.

On this particular Tuesday his customer was a young lady called Daisy, who was six years old and who had come to collect a pair of her father's boots which had seen long and active service in the road-sweeping business.

While Old Nolan was wrapping Daisy's father's boots, he quoted Plutarch to her, and was considerate enough to translate it from the Latin.

'"Only the wearer of the shoe knows where it pinches." So if your father could come in himself, Daisy . . .'

''E don't go nowhere no more,' explained Daisy.

'And why is that?'

''E won't.'

'Perhaps he has given you threepence for the repair?'

''E 'asn't.'

'Then next time you call?'

''E won't.'

'And why is that?'

'Because 'e can't. Stoopid! And 'oo's Plutarch when 'e's at 'ome?'

'A notable Roman.'

''Orrible foreigners!' exclaimed Daisy and spat on the floor.

Nolan held out his hand for the threepence, more from habit than from hope.

'Give yer twopence,' said Daisy.

'No.'

'Then yer'll 'ave ter wait till Fursday if yer wants the full fruppence.'

'Why Thursday, Daisy?'

Daisy turned on her heel pertly. ''Cos it comes arter Wednesday,' she said, and left the shop.

Disappointed but not dismayed, Nolan closed the money drawer, but then his eye was caught by something printed on the sheet of newspaper under the sheet in which he had wrapped Daisy's father's boots.

'Well, well, well,' he muttered to himself. 'Astonishing

. . . remarkable . . . astonishing . . . my hat and my coat directly . . .'

He took them from a hook and hurried out of the shop, only to return instantly, having forgotten to take with him the astonishing sheet of newspaper.

Chapter Five

In another and smarter part of the city was a milliner's shop. In order to prosper the shop needed to sell six hats a week, and it sold five. It did not prosper. The proprietress was Madame Fleur, who was also the manageress. She employed one saleswoman, a Mrs Joanna Tremaine, widow, the mother of Margaret and Gerald. If the saleswoman had been expert the shop would have sold at least six hats a week, and Madame Fleur might have been encouraged to pay her employee a proper wage. But she was not expert, Madame Fleur was not encouraged and Mrs Tremaine was paid a pittance. The less she was paid the more disgruntled she became, and the more disgruntled she became the fewer hats she sold.

At the very moment at which Old Nolan spotted the intriguing item in the newspaper, Mrs Tremaine, not entirely by mistake, poked a hat-pin into the head of a valued customer. That valued customer had stormed off into the street without buying a hat. Madame Fleur was understandably annoyed. She had frequently threatened to dismiss Mrs Tremaine, and would have done so, had she the slightest chance of finding anyone to replace her. So instead of giving her notice she announced that she would not give her the modest wages to which she was entitled, not until she had sold two more hats.

'If you were a little more courteous, Joanna . . .'

'They get what they deserve.'

'You thrust those pins into Mrs Gifford's head like a matador. I am truly at the end of my patience.'

Mrs Tremaine said nothing. The non-payment of the money due to her was a very serious matter, but her pride would not permit her to grovel for it. She was a good-looking woman of thirty-eight, but disappointment and deprivation made her appear older. She busied herself with rearranging the hats in the window. There were just three of these, and no amount of rearranging could make them glamorous or appealing. They were just hats, Joanna thought, and why anyone should want to spend money on them was beyond comprehension.

A half a mile away as the crow flies – though no self-respecting crow would care to venture into such dingy territory – was a miserable garret. At the window sat Margaret, trying to catch the last rays of the dying sun so that she could finish the pile of sewing in her lap. She had the air of a young woman rather than a girl, and a young woman used to hardship. Her brother Gerald, three years her junior, dark and aggressive, hated to see her working. It reminded him that he was not.

'That rubbishy old sewing! Put it away, Margaret,' he said.

'Only a few more stitches. Mother will be so disappointed if she comes home and it's not finished.'

'You're so dull.'

'I must not waste the light, Gerald. You know that.'

There was silence. Margaret continued to sew, and Gerald to kick the table. It was he who broke the silence to say in a wheedling voice:

'I want a kite. There's one in Ponsonby's shop. Give me threepence, Margaret.'

'I don't have threepence. You know I don't.'

'You have. It's in the box.' He referred to a wooden box high up on a shelf. 'I saw it there this morning.'

'It's for Mr Nolan. We owe it.'

'You'll have plenty of money when you take the sewing in, tomorrow. And Mr Nolan will wait.'

'He has waited too long already.'

The door opened and Joanna stepped slowly inside. She slumped in a chair and said nothing to her children; indeed she scarcely looked at them. Gerald went up to her and knelt by the chair. Absently she ran her fingers through his hair.

'Mama,' he said. 'There's a kite at Ponsonby's. It's three-pence. I want to buy it.'

'I told him no,' said Margaret.

Joanna looked crossly at her daughter. 'Margaret, how can you be so unkind? You know how few pleasures come Gerald's way.' She reached up and removed the threepence from the box. Gerald glanced triumphantly at Margaret.

'But, Mother, Mr Nolan . . .'

'Well, you must tell him he'll have it tomorrow. It's only money, Margaret.'

Without saying anything further, Margaret took from a bin a loaf of bread, and cut it into three slices. The outside slice, a little stale, she put aside for herself; the other slices

29

she spread thinly with butter and handed to her mother and brother. She poured three mugs of milk from a jug, leaving just enough for two smaller breakfast portions.

'How I wish, my dears, that you could have seen the way we used to live, Edward and I!' Margaret and Gerald exchanged glances, for this was a familiar tune. 'We never mentioned money. We just enjoyed ourselves. That it should come to this. Such a handsome man, your father. You take after him, Gerald.'

There was a tentative knock on the door. Gerald opened it and in some alarm Margaret recognised Nolan.

'Mrs Tremaine, good evening.' He held out his hand, then recalled that he was still wearing his hat, and removed it. 'Miss Tremaine . . . Master . . . erm . . .'

Gerald took Nolan's hat and placed it on his own head.

'Fine hat,' said Nolan. 'Suits you well. I have one much like it myself at home.'

'Why, Mr Nolan,' Joanna remarked with a strained smile, 'if you have come about the money for mending Gerald's boots . . .'

'Have I? No, I don't think I have. I mean, is there? Well, what is a few pence between friends?'

Margaret offered him her mug. 'Some milk, Mr Nolan?' But the cobbler, assessing the situation, declined. 'My liver,' he explained, putting his hand to where his kidneys were situated.

A silence followed. The three Tremaines waited for some clue as to why Nolan had visited them. They waited in vain.

'Well,' he said at last, 'this has really been most pleasant.'

Joanna could bear it no longer. 'But, Mr Nolan, why are you here?'

'Most extraordinary,' he said at once. 'And how I came

by it. Most remarkable.' Gerald giggled. Margaret grimaced at him to stop, but a smile was clearly evident upon her face also. Nolan glanced out of the tiny window through which at a distance the dome of St Paul's was visible with the setting sun behind it. 'My, my,' he said, 'the dome of St Paul's. The umbilicum, the belly-button, of the world.' This time even Margaret was unable to restrain her giggles. 'Now,' he said, 'the evidence,' and hunted through numerous pockets for the scrap of newspaper, and then for the spectacles through which to read it. Margaret took the cutting from him and read it through. She gasped and sat down heavily in the chair, before reading it aloud to the others:

Wanted: the next of kin of Edward John Tremaine, late a clerk in the National Bank. Apply Messrs Apted and Strange, Lincoln's Inn Fields, where they will learn something to their advantage.

'Is it good or bad, Mother?' asked Gerald.

'No change could be for the worse. Nonetheless . . .'

'Your husband was an Edward Tremaine, was he not?' said Nolan. 'Some things I forget, but the dates of the Roman emperors and the names of the dead husbands of my dear friends are etched into my memory.'

' "Something to our advantage" ', Margaret repeated, 'oh, Mother . . .' And she ran to where her mother was sitting and knelt to hug her. Gerald inserted himself between them. Tactfully Old Nolan withdrew, shutting the door quietly to avoid disturbing the touching scene, and only remembering an hour or so later that he had come away without his hat. But the evening was fine and he felt safe under the protection of the moonlit dome of St Paul's. His

31

lips moved as he muttered a short prayer for his impoverished friends. He prayed that good fortune be granted to them, and then he added a postscript that the good fortune would bring them happiness. He had lived too long to think that riches necessarily bring happiness, although he knew only too well that poverty rarely does.

Chapter Six

The following morning, their threadbare clothes smartened up as much as possible, mother, daughter and son presented themselves at the offices of Messrs Apted and Strange, Solicitors and Commissioners for Oaths. The brass plate outside their chambers shone brightly and suggested that, however murky the processes of the law, those who administer it are polished clean.

'Mother, why are they called solicitors?' Gerald wanted to know, but Joanna pretended not to hear this difficult question and fiddled with her children's clothes in an ecstasy of nervousness. Eventually she cleared her throat and said:

'Pull the bell, Margaret, and stand up straight, both of you. First impressions, you know.'

It was Cornelius Strange who welcomed the three of them into the chambers. He was almost as tall as the hatstand on which their coats were hung. He spoke endlessly of the weather as he led them into the presence of Mr Apted.

First Apted said he had to convince himself that they were who they claimed to be. He asked Joanna numerous questions about her late husband, but fortunately she had brought with her the one document which it was hard to dispute – her marriage certificate. Mr Apted studied this for some minutes, turning it over several times, as though expecting to find clues in the weave of the paper and the mysteries of the watermark which would only have significance to a man of the law. At last he appeared satisfied, and unburdened himself of the news which would change the lives of the three shabby creatures who stood before him.

'And so,' he concluded, 'it would appear that you, Master Gerald, are heir to the Tremaine estates. Not only will your circumstances change, so must your name. Henceforth you are no longer plain Gerald Tremaine, but Sir Gerald Tremaine, Baronet.'

There was a stunned silence. The grandfather clock continued to tick discreetly, reminding all clients of Apted and Strange that Time is Money, and that Accounts are to be Paid by Return, and it was almost possible to hear the dust gathering on the already dusty files. Once Joanna had regained her composure, her response was disappointing:

'Well, I'm sure we are most grateful to you, Mr Apted, but what I need to know is when will Lady Tremaine be vacating the house?'

'Mother!' cried Margaret, astonished at her mother's callousness.

'Well, these things must be faced and planned for, my dear. There's no running away from life's realities.'

There will be sparks struck when Lady Tremaine and Mrs Tremaine come face to face, thought Mr Apted, but then wouldn't there be fat fees for a family solicitor acting for both sides of the same family? He thought of the silver chafing dish which he could buy with the money he was likely to make out of such a situation, resolving that his wife and children would get none of the money. The previous evening they had taken the seat out of the chair as he was about to sit down to dinner and he had fallen through it. Instead of carving the mutton he had had to beg them to help him up. He replied to Joanna's question:

'I hope it is not too severe a disappointment to you, Madam, but under the terms of Sir Nicholas's will Lady Tremaine is a life tenant in Trecastle House and may not be removed. However, she is generously prepared to share her home with you and your children.'

'But Mother, it will be wonderful!' Margaret cried, unable to remain silent any longer. 'And Gerald a baronet!'

'Wonderful? Guests in Gerald's house?'

'*Our* house,' said Gerald.

'I have here the necessary documents prepared for signature,' said Apted, producing them, 'and when you are ready I shall have Mr Strange come in as a witness.'

Joanna cleared her throat delicately. 'Perhaps there is something else you have omitted to mention, Mr Apted?'

Money was what she meant, and money was what Mr Apted went on to discuss. There was money for them, and a great deal of it, but unfortunately he was not in a position to advance them any just now. Although he had no doubts as to the validity of their claim, it still had to be legally confirmed, and that would involve much scratching of pens on parchment, and further fat fees for solicitors. Mrs Tremaine wheedled and bullied, argued and threatened, but to no avail.

'Well, really!' Joanna stormed, casting a murderous look

at the ancient buildings. If she had a trumpet, Gerald felt, she would march us round and round the place until the walls came down. But then she had a brainwave.

*   *   *

Madame Fleur was furious. Joanna might be bad-tempered and discourteous at times, she might discourage the customers, and even stick hat-pins into their heads, but until today she had always turned up. Without an assistant there could be none of those little lunchtime visits to the *Bear and Staff*, from which she would return, eyes brighter, mind clearer and nose a little redder; none of those little visits without which she really did not know how a woman in her delicate condition – she suffered dreadfully from 'the vapours' – could be expected to survive.

Just then the bell pinged and who should be standing there but her employee with her two horrid children. Madame Fleur was dumbfounded. What new kind of insolence was this?

'Mrs Tremaine!' she cried. 'What in the name of all that's holy do you mean by this behaviour? Where have you been? What have you been thinking of?'

'I am thinking of handing in my notice. I am also thinking of buying a hat. This one!' And she picked up the most elaborate and expensive model in the shop, a hat bedecked with a colourful variety of flowers and fruit, and placed it beguilingly upon her head. 'What do you think, Margaret? *C'est moi?*' She tilted it a little one way and then the other. '*Voilà!*'

Margaret did not trust herself to speak. She wished that a trap-door would gape open in front of her and carry her down to decent obscurity. Gerald said:

'It really suits you, Mama.'

Joanna turned to Madame Fleur and handed her the hat. 'Be so good as to box it for me and send the account to my cousin Lady Tremaine, of Trecastle House, Cornwall. Our circumstances, you see, have changed.'

'It's true, Madame Fleur,' said Margaret. 'And Gerald's a baronet. The solicitor told us.'

It was a good deal for the proprietor of a small hat-shop to take in, but a sale was a sale, and now she would never have to pay Joanna her wages. At least she could afford to shut up shop for a half an hour and enjoy the familiar comforts of the *Bear and Staff*.

'Very well,' she said at length.

'Very well, what?'

This was too much, even in the cause of profit. Madame Fleur looked Joanna full in the face. 'I will not call you "Madam"!'

'In that case,' Joanna announced triumphantly, 'I shall buy my hats elsewhere.' With that she thrust the fruity and flowery hat into the arms of the enraged Madame Fleur, and flounced out, followed by the young baronet. Margaret lingered for a moment as if she wished to say something friendly, but she could find no suitable words, and made do with a smile.

*　　　*　　　*

The garret was cramped with many parcels, the floor littered with brightly coloured wrapping paper and string. After the visit to the milliner's, Joanna had taken them to Fleet Street, where she had bought dresses and hats, lingerie and shoes, instructing the shopkeepers to 'send the account to my cousin, Lady Tremaine of Trecastle House,

Cornwall', and they had been happy to oblige her. Margaret had refused to let her mother buy anything for her and, as a result, was accused of being a killjoy. But, unknown to Margaret, Joanna bought some ribbons, and secretly the girl was delighted when these were presented to her once they reached home, even though she felt like the accessory to a crime.

'It *is* wrong of us, Mother. I've no chance to return the sewing, and so we still have no money to pay poor Mr Nolan.'

At which point there was a knock at the door, and Joanna remarked that, if it was Mr Nolan, he should he told to send the account to Lady Tremaine. Gerald laughed raucously as Margaret did indeed show Mr Nolan in.

'The news is good?' he inquired, and then caught sight of the parcels. 'Indeed I see that the news is very good indeed. *Mutatis mutandis*, my dear friends, I rejoice in your good fortune.'

Overcome, Margaret hugged him. 'Had it not been for you, dear Mr Nolan,' she said, 'you and your sharp eyes . . .'

'Do you like my kite?' asked Gerald. 'And did you know that I have become a baronet?'

'Have you now?'

'Not that I quite know what a baronet is. But now that I am one, I expect I shall find out.'

Nolan coughed discreetly. 'Perhaps I may be permitted to mention,' he said, 'that I have worked for the Lord Mayor's first cousin and gave him satisfaction. It will be an honour to measure the baronet for anything from slippers to Wellington boots.'

Joanna said: 'Sadly that will not be possible, Mr Nolan, for we are shortly to take up residence on the Trecastle estates in Cornwall.'

'You will come and visit us, Mr Nolan,' said Margaret, taking hold of his hand, 'for we shall need good advice, I'm sure, and we may not easily come by it in Cornwall.'

'Yes, do come, Nolan,' added Gerald in a haughty voice, 'we shall be delighted to entertain you.'

'I don't know what to say.'

'Then say nothing,' said Margaret, 'just promise.'

'Promises are cheap,' said Nolan sadly, for not only was he to lose his friends, but it seemed as though he would not be making Wellington boots for the baronet either. 'And as for good advice, it's not so much a matter of giving it – anyone can do that – as taking it. But may God go with you all, as I am sure He will.'

Nolan might have added much more, for, once he got into the groove it was not easy to shake him out of it, but Gerald interrupted him.

'A kite's no good in London,' he said, 'but in Cornwall . . . Do you think baronets are allowed them?'

Chapter Seven

It was the letter from Lady Tremaine which, more than anything else, brought home to Joanna that she was not living in a dream, and that the new frocks and hats, the new lingerie and shoes, would not vanish with the morning light. It was a handsome letter. The paper was of the finest and faintly scented. The handwriting was an educated copperplate, and the address, Trecastle House, Trecastle, Cornwall, was a sight for sore eyes!

Joanna remembered when Edward, her husband, had spoken of his Cornish relatives. He had mentioned the height of the ceilings and the peacocks in the garden. He had spoken of a gloomy butler and wistaria climbing around an old stable yard. Whatever else he may have remembered she could not now recall. He had been dead these eight years.

Once they were safely in the privacy of the luxurious first class compartment on the little train which puffed its way sedately through Surrey and Hampshire, Joanna took the letter once more from her handbag. She read it to Margaret and Gerald.

Trecastle House
Trecastle
Cornwall
July 17th 1880

Dear Mrs Tremaine,

Please believe me when I say that the news I have received from Mr Apted has given me nothing but pleasure. Since the death of my husband I had believed myself quite alone in the world. It is no small consolation to me to learn that the fine old name of Tremaine shall live on to bring yet more honour to the British Navy and glory to our dear Queen and her possessions overseas.

The House on the Cliff stands ready to welcome its new master. It belongs entirely to Gerald; all it contains is his. I am confident that he will be worthy his great inheritance and I feel that I love him already because God has sent him in my little Nico's place. The welcome will be yours too and Miss Tremaine's. I long once more to hear the voice of children in these echoing corridors.

Yours truly,
the Dowager (as I most willingly call myself)
Lady Tremaine.

'She says nothing about kites,' said Gerald.

Margaret was staring out of the window. Sheep, cows and horses in the fields to her were sights as rare as diamonds. She had seen such things in picture books; she could not understand why Joanna and Gerald did not share her excitement. Perhaps they had been so busy in packing up all her mother's newly acquired possessions that they had not properly considered the extraordinary change that was about to come over their life. Margaret had had less to pack, but she had not forgotten a small and slightly chipped porcelain statue of the Virgin Mary. It was the only present her father had given her which she still possessed, and her greatest treasure.

'Gerald,' said Joanna, leaning forward and touching her son on the knee, 'you must be prepared for a grand welcome.'

'Will there be bands playing?'

'I should not be at all surprised. And certainly there will be a reception committee. Triumphal arches too, most probably. If the village children perform something for us you must promise not to yawn or be rude.'

'Mama, really,' said Gerald in a weary voice, 'I *do* know how to behave.'

*　　　*　　　*

At Trecastle Village station, the reception committee consisted of two fat old horses and an antique carriage much in need of restoration. (It had not been used since William Randle took it to Penzance.) What they said in the village about the new arrivals was summed up in the words of Jack Austen, window-cleaner and chimney-sweep, to the landlord of the *Dun Cow*:

'We're honest men, if we're anything at all, and we ain't a-going to pretend what we can't feel. It would not be decent like to the memory of them as is gone.'

Lounging across the street from the platform were Joe Snell and Tom Austen, Jack's boy, both more or less Gerald's age, and scornful.

'What be his name then?' asked Joe.

'Gerald.'

'What kind of name be that, Tom?'

''Tain't English.'

'Tremaines was always Nicholas or Walter.'

'Aye, or Joseph. Sometimes they was Joseph.'

'Aye.'

'*Gerald*? That's no kind of a name at all, Tom.' And Joe spat in the ditch, aiming at a stinging nettle and hitting it fair and square.

''Tain't English,' said Tom.

''Tain't Rooshian neither, an' it ain't French.'

'Maybe it's Dutch, Joe.'

'Aye, Dutch for sure,' said Joe, delighted that the matter had been resolved.

By now the steam from the train was visible from the far side of the hill, and the boys' sharp ears could pick out the puffing of the engine. Tom plucked a stalk of grass and sucked the white juice from the end of it. The train pulled into the station.

The next five minutes were not pleasant ones for Joanna. The guard put out her numerous pieces of luggage and not one of the onlookers stepped forward to help her. One thing they knew how to do, she thought, and that was to stare. She clapped her hands, and an old porter came ambling along, as if their arrival was of no more interest than a sea-gull settling on the roof of the stationmaster's hut. As for the carriage, it was beyond belief.

'Well, really!' Joanna gasped.

'I say, they're a pack of duffers here,' said Gerald. 'I wish we'd stayed in London and lived in a big house and not come to this stupid place.'

These remarks, overheard by Joe and Tom, most definitely did not meet with their approval. Margaret, embarrassed as so often in the company of her family, did her best to repair things.

'Were it not for the deaths of four people, all no doubt loved in this village, we should not be here at all.'

At this the stationmaster and the porter exchanged approving glances. Joanna meanwhile had advanced to the carriage, and stood grimly in front of the coachman, hands on hips. Flies buzzed round the horses' heads. The coachman packed tobacco into his pipe. The scent of cow parsley filled the air, mingling with the sweat of the horses, and the faint but unmistakable smell of the sea. Joe Snell whistled tunelessly an irritating phrase over and over. At length the coachman climbed down from the box to help the reluctant porter load the luggage.

When the carriage finally pulled away, the stationmaster turned to the porter and said:

''Tis a sad day for Trecastle.'

'He's Dutch,' said Joe authoritatively.

'Aye, I thought as much,' said the porter.

Chapter Eight

Margaret woke and stretched. It was very odd. She was lying between sheets, which were stiff and cool and faintly scented and the colour of cream. No matter how she stretched, her toes came into contact with nothing, just more and more sheets. She tried stretching her arms and opening her fingers. The bed, which seemed to have no bottom to it, apparently had no edges either. To resolve the mystery of where she was she opened her eyes.

She saw a maid bending over the fire-grate. That was even odder. She did not know of course that she was a maid, or very clearly what a maid was. When the maid heard her stir, she turned towards her, smiled, bobbed a curtsey, smiled again, wished her good morning and departed.

The fire crackled cheerfully. A fire in August, whatever next? The maid brought in a breakfast tray, covered with a damask cloth. She explained that since Miss Tremaine was probably a little tired after her journey she had brought her breakfast in bed. She hoped everything was to Miss Tremaine's satisfaction.

It certainly was. Satisfaction scarcely described what Margaret felt. It was rather as if she had stepped straight into one of those coloured illustrations that adorned the front of the books they had at school. She climbed out of bed, pausing to admire the long linen nightgown which she could not remember having climbed into, and then made a circuit of the room, touching everything with the tips of her fingers as though blessing them. On the chimney piece was the beautiful porcelain Madonna. On the wall a collection of miniatures; handsome lords and ladies delicately painted on ivory. On the floor was a rug woven from Indian silk, with an intricate pattern of leaves and flowers and huntsmen and dogs leaping through the undergrowth.

She moved to the window. In the foreground she saw the lawn, and a sunken garden of roses sheltered by box hedges; in the middle distance a park with sweet chestnut trees; far away, a shimmer of sea. Then she returned to the breakfast tray: crisp white bread and creamy butter; a pear on a plate and an ivory-handled knife to cut it with; a generous pile of scrambled egg sprinkled with fresh parsley. And, best of all, in a tall tumbler was as much milk as she could possibly drink.

But for a while she neither ate nor drank. It was too much, it overwhelmed her. She rested her head on one of the four pillows – it was the softest of pillows and comfortingly cool against her cheek – and let the tears flow. Having cried for a bit she felt extremely hungry and polished off everything on the tray.

An hour later she was walking in the garden when a peacock strutted up to her and opened its tail in a brilliantly coloured fan.

'Oh, thank you,' she whispered.

Joanna's breakfast had not been so peaceful. Lady Tremaine was not in evidence, nor were any servants, with the exception of old Robinson. Joanna wanted to know where the footmen were, and the maids. Respectfully, Robinson coughed and explained that in the best houses it was customary for the butler alone to wait at the breakfast table. Thereupon Joanna complained that the toast was burnt, which it wasn't; but it had been necessary to complain about something on her first morning, or the butler would never take her seriously.

Gerald had announced that he wanted a pony, and had asked Robinson whether there was not one in the stables. Robinson had avoided the question, at which Gerald had muttered that if being a baronet meant that nobody would give him a straight answer, then he did not care much for it, and if Robinson would not answer his questions he would ask Lady Tremaine instead. He liked the old girl, he said, although he had only met her briefly when they arrived at the house. He was sure she would let him have a pony at once.

While he spoke he played with a dish of wax fruit, which was marvellously life-like. He juggled with two wax apples and a wax pear, and he dropped one of the pears. Bending down with some difficulty, Robinson retrieved it and removed the dish from Gerald's reach. Joanna smiled adoringly at Gerald's playfulness.

There was a tap at the door, which opened a crack to admit Tom Austen from the village. Tom was about Gerald's age but growing fast. He was wearing his Sunday best, but the suit was short and tight at the wrists and ankles. Tom held his cap in his hand and was twisting it nervously. This was a very different Tom from the self-confident lounger who had watched the newcomers arrive at Trecastle Station.

'Robinson, who is this?' Joanna asked with distaste. Tom glanced at his shoes in case he had brought something unpleasant into the house. They seemed clean enough.

'If you please, ma'am, I be Tom Austen, ma'am.' He glanced inside his hat, for he had the words of his speech written on a piece of paper which he had concealed there. 'And I have been instructed to show the young Master and Miss Tremaine round the village.'

'Is there a pony in the stable, Tom?' asked Gerald.

'Why, yes, but –'

'Then I shall have it. You must wait while I talk to Lady Tremaine.'

Robinson was still wondering how best to dissuade young Gerald from any such course of action when the boy was out of the room and halfway up the stairs. There he halted and gazed again at the portrait of Nicolas Tremaine whom he had replaced. He disliked the boy's ringlets and the prettified expression on the boy's face, but that was the way of pictures. They made things look the way people wanted them to look, not the way things really looked. Despite the ringlets, Gerald thought to himself that he would like to have known Nicholas, to have had a cousin, even one who wore ringlets and a cocked hat. They could have climbed the cliffs together.

Chapter Nine

Imagining himself to be climbing the cliffs, he struggled up the rest of the stairs until, flushed with triumph, he burst into Lady Tremaine's bedroom. She was sitting up in bed with a breakfast tray in front of her, and she looked, Gerald thought, like the Queen. Alarmed by the boy's unexpected appearance she choked on a piece of toast and put a hand to her heart.

'Goodness gracious!' she gasped when she had regained her composure. 'Has the house taken fire?'

'Why did he wear a cocked hat?'

'No, no, no, no!' Lady Tremaine wagged the remaining piece of toast at him severely. 'This will not do at all. Move more slowly, Gerald darling, and speak more gently. I am neither deaf nor a half mile away.'

'Well, why?'

'Because he used to call himself Nico, a little lad, and tell the world that one day he would be a famous sailor and wear a cocked hat.'

'I wish he were here.'

'If wishes were horses, beggars would ride. Come here and give me a kiss.'

Gerald, who had lived in a house full of women for far too long, was not much of a one for kissing, but Lady Tremaine was powdered so smoothly and scented so sweetly that kissing her was not unlike eating an ice-cream, and he quite liked it.

Satisfied with the kiss, Lady Tremaine wiped delicately at the corners of her mouth with the damask table-napkin, and instructed:

'You may call me Grandmama. That is what Nico called me.'

'Is it nice living so long, Grandmama?' Gerald asked.

Lady Tremaine sighed deeply. It was a difficult question. There were mornings when she opened her eyes in dread of a new day, and nights when she closed them in happy expectation of an endless sleep.

'It will be better,' she said, 'now that you have come to share my life.'

'I shall be a sailor,' said Gerald, 'and wear a cocked hat and kill Frenchies with my bare hands, but first I shall make them beg me for mercy and then I shall kill them anyway. Nico drowned, Grandmama, didn't he?'

The old lady sighed again, but gave no answer.

'I want a pony to ride,' said Gerald. 'One of my own. I want it more than anything. And Tom Austen said that there is one in the stable, so why should I not ride that one?'

'You shall have one of your own, but you shall not have that one, and I shall explain to you why.' At which Lady Tremaine patted the bed next to where she lay and Gerald sat down, his back against a mountain of pillows.

Lady Tremaine passed him a silver dish full of buttery toast. Gerald looked suspiciously at it; there were no crusts! What sort of bread was that? He would not trust it if it were the last piece of toast on earth.

'My husband went to the Moor and chose Peterkin from amongst twenty other ponies, and, when we heard the sad news, he said that he would keep Peterkin for a time in case our own little Nico came home. But he never came home. And my husband still insisted that no one else was to have or ride the pony, and no one else has, but his tackle has been kept shining until the day on which the heir to Trecastle returns from his watery grave.'

Quite gently Gerald said: 'If I am not to have Peterkin, may I have one like him?'

'You shall have the nearest thing to him that Helston market can supply.'

When Joanna heard about this she was furious. If Gerald were master in the house and if everything in the house and on the estate belonged to him, then what was all this about Peterkin? All he had to do was ride the pony, and Lady T. could gnash her teeth all she liked. But Joanna was displeased and amazed when Gerald insisted that in this matter Lady Tremaine was perfectly reasonable and he had no intention of going against her wishes.

'Sentimental twaddle!' cried Joanna, but she had lost that particular argument and well she knew it.

Chapter Ten

Proud as he was of his village, Tom Austen was shy when it came to showing it off. He wanted Gerald and Margaret to admire it, but he did not want them to share it. So he made a rather surly guide until some particular treasure fired his enthusiasm, and he could not contain himself. Then, ashamed of having given himself away, he would become surly once again.

Trecastle was two villages, a village around a green, and a village around a harbour, but it bore just the single name. To travel from the green to the harbour involved a steep climb down a path part of which was cut straight through an outcrop of rock; this tunnel was excellent for echoes, and Tom stamped his feet several times as he passed through. Then suddenly:

'Are you Dutch?' he asked.

'Who says I am?' Gerald countered fiercely.

'There's rumours.'

'Well, start another rumour, Tom, that I'll break the head of anyone who says I am. And I will too.'

Margaret asked where the other children were. They had seen none since they left the big house.

'In school,' said Tom, and added that he did not think much of the person who could ask such an obvious question.

'But you're not.'

'They give me the day off,' Tom explained, 'to show you two round. Any ways up, I set no store by book-learning.'

They had reached the harbour where men and women were sitting on the sand mending nets. The smell was rich and tangy with seaweed and creosote, rotting tar and salty air mixed in a breath-taking aroma. Tom drew it in with a deep breath, then pointed at the jetty and the bobbing sails:

'There's all I need to know. The spring tides and the mackerel shoals and the Lizard rocks. You see that little beauty there?' Shading his eyes he directed their attention to a small fishing boat rearing and bucking in the moderate swell. 'She'll be mine one day an' I shall paint her green.'

Margaret said: 'I have seen the sea before. At Margate. Father took me for the day. There was a Punch and Judy. He said Judy deserved all she got. Gerald was too little to come.'

'I dreamt of the sea though,' said Gerald. 'Almost every night.'

A little way along the jetty in front of the coastguard's station William Randle sat at his easel. He was a familiar figure and tolerated by the fishermen. There had been a day, some three years past, when William Randle had sold a seascape to a visiting American, who had handed him such a large sum of money that even the fishermen were impressed. But as the seasons came and went, and William sold no more pictures, it was now generally considered that the American had been much like the freakish sky-blue lobster which Tom's father had found in his pots and which had also been the talk of the little village.

Tom introduced Randle to the two young Tremaines, and Randle remarked politely that he was pleased to meet them.

'What are you doing, Randle?' Gerald asked in the grand voice that he often used now he was a baronet.

'I'm painting,' said Randle. 'At least I'm trying to paint.' He grinned attractively. 'At least my name is on the bottom of my pictures.'

Gerald glanced at the canvas. The sea, he thought, looked rather solid, and the boats rather curiously shaped, so he asked:

'Is this one of your best?'

'It's charming,' said Margaret, who thought that it was.

'I know it is,' said Randle gloomily. 'It wasn't meant to be.'

'It was you,' Gerald announced, 'who painted Nicholas in his cocked hat.'

'I know.'

'Will you paint me in one?'

'No,' said Randle after a pause. 'I don't think I can do that.'

Gerald turned to Margaret and said pettishly:

'I don't see the point in being a baronet if no one will do as they're told.'

Randle painted a bit more blue on to the sky, then wiped it off again with a rag.

'I'll gladly paint your picture. But not in a cocked hat. You see, Sir Gerald, Nico's father was my dearest friend, and I was godfather to his little lad.'

'It's stupid!' said Gerald. 'I don't understand it and I don't much want to.'

Margaret felt ashamed for him. She said: 'We're all very sad that our cousin died. We would never have wished our good fortune at such a price.'

'I would have liked the good fortune and Nico here too,' said Gerald, reasonably enough.

'We just manage with what God has given us,' said Randle, and sighed again. 'I would have liked the genius of a Michelangelo, but all I do is paint.'

Tom pointed out to sea to his father's fishing boat.

'You can paint that boat when it's mine,' he said graciously.

'Thank you,' said William Randle.

'Green. You should do real work.'

'I should.'

'Anyone can paint pictures!'

And with that Tom was off to 'do real work', which in his case meant lying on his back in the long grass and counting the clouds.

Margaret thought the artist was probably the most handsome man she had ever met, and she felt self-conscious. If she had known that she would be meeting him, she would have taken more trouble with her hair, would have chosen a prettier frock, would have . . . Randle was explaining to them both about his friendship with Nico's father, Walter. They had been at school together, had shared an interest in fishing and birds, and William had often spent his summers at Trecastle.

'Later,' he said, 'when I wanted so much to paint, Walter's parents let me use one of the empty cottages on the estate, and it was in return for that kindness that I painted

Nico's portrait.'

'And after his death they wanted you to stay?' Margaret asked. 'To remind them of their son?'

Randle looked at her sharply, at her fiercely intelligent eyes which gave colour and character to a face which was conventionally pretty rather than beautiful.

'You know a great deal about adult matters, young lady,' he said.

'She's blushing!' cried Gerald infuriatingly. And Margaret found herself putting a hand to her cheek, which did indeed feel warm to the touch. Then – for he really did like the artist – Gerald added in a lordly manner: 'Why not come to dinner this evening, Mr Randle? I shall have a word with Cook.'

'Do come,' Margaret added. 'Mother would enjoy it so.'

'I shall be honoured to accept.'

Chapter Eleven

He really was the prettiest and sleekest of ponies. He had a look in his eye which seemed to say: Yes, I am a very special pony, so don't take liberties with me!

On the way back from the harbour Gerald spotted him cropping grass in the paddock and was struck dumb with delight. He sat and stared until Joe Snell emerged from the stables, chewing a piece of straw with cool insolence. Finding his tongue (which was never lost for long), Gerald announced to his sister that this was the pony for him, to which Margaret replied that most likely he belonged to someone else.

'He does,' said Gerald. 'He belonged to Nicholas, and Lady Tremaine says that she will on no account part with him, and that no one must ride him until Nico comes home, which of course he never will. But maybe she will sell him to me. She likes me, you see, and she may not have too much money now that I have everything.'

It was at this point that Joe Snell intervened and said that Peterkin was absolutely not for sale, not if Gerald owned the whole of Cornwall.

''E won't be sold on account of 'e can't be sold an' 'e can't be sold on account of the young master's been dead these many years. So there.' With which he handed the pony some sugar from a parcel and pulled his fine big ears. 'Here, Peterkin, you shall have your sugar an' nobody else be a-goin' to take you, not while Joe's around.'

'Joe Snell,' said Gerald. 'I have a mind to ride Peterkin anyway. Fetch his saddle.'

'Not if you was King of England,' said Joe, 'which you ain't, not by a long chalk.'

Gerald wasted no time. He aimed a blow at Joe's chest, which Joe dodged easily enough. The two boys were evenly matched, Gerald a little taller than Joe with a longer reach, but Joe more sinewy and muscular. As Joe rolled up his sleeves in a businesslike way, Margaret begged Gerald to let the matter rest. Brawling with a village boy was a terrible way for a new baronet to begin.

'Not if I thrash him, though,' said Gerald.

At which moment Tom Austen appeared on the scene and took up a position next to Joe.

'Problems, Joe?' he asked. But Joe insisted that he was perfectly capable of handling them himself.

'There's two of us now, Dutchie, and all you've got is your sister,' said Tom.

But Margaret, muttering about how childish they were all being, was already on her way back to the big house. Gerald, reckoning that the odds had changed against him, decided that the moment for heroics had passed. As he followed his sister, his parting shot was:

'I shall have Peterkin. I can get what I want from

Grandmama. You'll see!'

'Grandmama! Grandmama!' yelled Tom and Joe in unison, but they feared the worst. Boy against boy, they fancied their chances against any number of Geralds, but when it came to a matter of crossing Lady T. they knew their limitations.

Joe used the rudest word he knew, which made him feel good. And Tom used the rudest word *he* knew which made Joe feel even better, because Tom's word was clearly not as rude a word as Joe's word, and when you only know a few rude words such matters count for a good deal.

And then they all went home for tea.

But in the matter of Peterkin, Gerald was not able to have his way, and Robinson returned from Helston market with a pony which, though not quite as perfect as Peterkin, was extremely charming. Gerald rode Dandy – for that was the new pony's name – most fearlessly about the countryside. Tom and Joe and the rest of the villagers were given a solemn lecture by Robinson, who told them that it was Lady Tremaine's especial wish that they be civil to the young baronet, and they did their best. Even Joe was persuaded to take off his cap when Gerald rode by on Dandy, but after he was out of earshot Joe would mutter:

'Compare that *thing* with Peterkin! Why, 'e ain't fit to hold a candle to him, and 'e ain't getting no sugar lumps out of me, an' that's a fact!'

And the long summer days passed and the fields were full of buttercups and celandines.

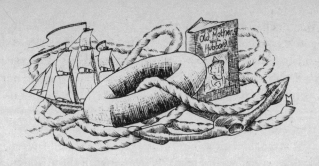

Chapter Twelve

One day there was a great upheaval when Lady Tremaine moved into the Dower House. She took with her only her personal possessions and the portrait of Nico in the cocked hat. Her much-loved maid, Dulcie, accompanied her, but when Robinson spoke of coming too, Lady Tremaine would have none of it. She took him to the window.

'Tell me what you see,' she said.

'Why, the lawn, my lady, the sunken garden, the oak tree . . .'

'And what if I were to instruct the gardener to dig up the oak and transplant it?'

'He would try to persuade you against such a terrible thing.'

'And if I persisted?'

'Why, my lady, the tree would die.'

'Indeed it would,' said Lady Tremaine, 'for its roots run

very deep. And so do yours. You are to stay put, Robinson, and serve the new mistress.' There was a hint of a twinkle in her old eyes as she added: 'And teach her our ways.'

'I shall endeavour to give satisfaction, my lady,' said Robinson. He often said that, and always lived up to it.

Joanna was delighted to see Lady Tremaine go, although later she felt a strange sense of loss.

It was a day or two later that Joanna came upon William Randle at his easel. He was scowling with dissatisfaction. He could not help wondering why, when there must be many things which he did well, he persisted in doing the one thing which he did badly. Joanna came and stood behind him, and watched while he painted a bird into a large expanse of sky and then painted it out again.

'I liked that bird,' said Joanna. 'I have been wondering, William, whether you would consider painting my portrait to hang alongside my ancestors.'

Ancestors by marriage, William thought to himself, but said that of course he would be delighted. Joanna did a little twirl of pleasure, a twirl which showed off her new dress to the best advantage. Then William had to spoil it all by adding: 'But I must confess that I was planning to ask you if I might paint your daughter.'

'Of course, but she will have to take her turn.'

'A young girl's beauty passes so quickly. It would be a pity, would it not, to fail to catch her at just this moment?'

Would it be a pity? Joanna found it hard to decide. Instead she said:

'Yes, she is lovely, is she not? They say she takes after me.'

It was soon after this conversation with Joanna that William decided to go abroad. He had been considering a change of scene for some time and he had recently heard that French subjects were all the rage in the London galleries. He would go to Brittany in the north-west of France. He would join the Pont-Aven group of painters. He would work as he had never worked before, and return in triumph to exhibit at the Academy. He would be rich and wear a velvet jacket. He would return to Trecastle in triumph and found a Cornish School of Painting. Young artists would come to Trecastle and ask his advice on technical matters. He would be buried in Westminster Abbey with trumpets.

To everybody's surprise – and even to his own – no sooner had he announced his intention of going to Brittany than he upped and went.

So Lady Tremaine and Dulcie moved and so did William Randle. But Joanna and Margaret and Gerald remained in their new home, and Robinson stayed put too, and gently attempted to teach them the old way of doing things, which some think is the only way of doing things. Of the four perhaps only Robinson was content.

Joanna had everything she had ever dreamed of having, more indeed than she had ever had in the happy days of her early marriage. But there was something in her which made her bad-tempered and snappish, and knowing that she had no cause to be snappish caused her to be even more snappish. Gerald too had caught this discontent from his mother in the way one catches an infection; he had been too close to her for too long. So he strode around the house and the village as though both belonged to him, which of course they did. Only when he visited Lady Tremaine in the Dower House did he feel that he could relax and be himself. They often played cribbage together, and told each other their dreams. The old woman and the young boy forged a link which could not be broken. She loved him as the son and grandson she had lost. He loved her as the grandmother he had never had.

Margaret might have been happy. She loved the house and the village and the way the sun sparkled on the waves and the way the sea was always changing colour. In her quiet way she also loved William, or at least she loved looking at him, which is the beginning of love. But she was not happy because she felt guilty about so many things. At least she found comfort in writing a long letter to Mr Nolan, enclosing the money they owed him. That at least was one thing she no longer had to feel guilty about.

When Nolan received the letter, he was so pleased that he folded it away and put it in his pocket to be read later. That is the best thing to do with letters from friends. In the case of Mr Nolan it has to be said that he quite forgot that he had ever received and concealed the letter, and it was some days later that he discovered it and could not for the life of him imagine how it could have got there. The last part of the letter was the part that pleased Nolan best:

'I do miss your shop, indeed I do,' Margaret had written, 'and you in it and the moon gleaming on the dome of St Paul's. Glance at it as you read this, Mr Nolan, and wish us all well.'

And Nolan did glance at the dome as instructed and the moon was gleaming as it should. He muttered a prayer for Margaret and blessed her for remembering him, and blessed all innocent people; which was an irony really, for Mr Nolan was about as innocent himself as a man can be.

Chapter Thirteen

Near the town and harbour of Brest, where the ships of the French Navy stand at anchor, there is a small fishing village called Plougastel. It was never much of a place, but it was more of a place at the time of which I write than it is today. There is an old church at the top of a hill, and a churchyard with a carved stone Calvary. Sailors would look out for this, for it spoke to them of courage in danger, of hope and of safety.

The harbour was not unlike the harbour at Trecastle, but Plougastel had a beach which Trecastle did not, and a particularly pleasant beach it was too, sheltered and sandy. It was the perfect beach for lying on and thinking in the sunshine of all the important things you ought to be doing instead.

On this beach stood a tall red-bearded Englishman with a note-pad and a pencil. In front of him was a little girl dressed in a dark frock and a red bodice laced up the front.

She had a quaint shawl and an embroidered apron and a tight-fitting multi-coloured cap, adorned with gold and silver lace and fastened under her chin. She was as pretty as a picture, which means a good deal prettier than the picture which William Randle – for, of course, it was he – was preparing to paint of her. Her name was Lucie Gouarhne.

Feeling that she had stood still quite long enough, Lucie came running round to have a look at the fruits of all William's efforts. Though secretly a little disappointed, she was still generous enough to say:

'*C'est bien, Monsieur.*'

And when he insisted that it was not at all *bien*, Lucie ran off to fetch a group of her friends who crowded round and said it was indeed *bien*, and that William was extremely clever *for an Englishman*. Anxious to change the subject, William took a hard-boiled egg from his lunch-basket and began to produce it from here, there and everywhere, from this child's ear, from this child's mouth, and from this child's sleeve. The children were delighted. There is nothing quite like discovering that your sleeve, which you felt sure contained an arm, contains an egg as well. William had just reached out to pluck the egg from behind the head of a pale, quiet boy, when he froze momentarily, as someone freezes who sees a ghost.

The cries of the children: '*M'sieur, M'sieur . . . de plus . . . encore . . . faites vos jeux avec moi . . . avec moi . . . moi . . .*' brought him back to his senses, but he had lost his appetite for conjuring tricks, and wished to be left alone to think. They left him alone at last. He sat on the harbour wall thinking and eating his hard-boiled egg.

That pale, quiet boy had reminded him of somebody, a boy whom he had painted as a favour to the boy's father, his best friend. But of course this boy was considerably older than that boy, and in any case that boy was dead, had died in a dreadful accident, a drowning with his . . . Wait. If that boy had lived he would now be just about the age of this boy.

Putting down what remained of his hard-boiled egg, William picked up his sketch pad and turned to a fresh page. He made a preliminary sketch of the pale, quiet boy, and then added a cocked hat. No! It was a trick of memory, a stupid coincidence, a meaningless likeness, which only an artist, sensitive to such things, would have made anything of. He tried again. Again the pale, quiet boy turned into young Sir Nicholas. He was so startled by this that he quite forgot his hard-boiled egg, and set off to find Lucie and the other children.

He did not find them that afternoon. It was a religious feast day, and they were all in church. He could not find them the following day until after school. He overtook Lucie as she climbed up the hill in her wooden shoes, singing snatches of an old Breton song in her piping voice.

'Lucie! At last,' said William, with a broad grin on his face. 'I thought I'd lost you.'

'*Monsieur?*'

'I need your help.' William took from his pocket a rather crumpled page from his sketch book. It was crumpled because he had already shown it to the priest, and the grocer, and the baker, and a number of strangers, none of whom had been helpful at all. 'Here. This boy? Where do I find this boy?'

'*Monsieur?*'

'Oh lord, why do you not speak English like civilised people?'

'*Monsieur?*'

'This boy. *Où? Où?*'

It sounded as though the handsome Englishman was in some pain, and Lucie could not suppress a smile. But she understood at last what he wanted.

'*Azicklezad. Vous cherchez Azicklezad, Monsieur. Venez!*'

'I beg your pardon?'

'*Azicklezad. Venez!*'

Since William still seemed slow to comprehend, Lucie took his hand and led him up the hill. At last she stopped before a low building with a thatched roof that was level with the top of the door. Two or three chickens came clucking out as she led him in.

The interior consisted of just two rooms, divided by a hanging curtain. The floor was earth, trodden down, but in places rather bumpy, the sort of room in which it would be frustrating to play marbles. The furniture was a wooden table and three wooden benches. In the corner were two fold-away beds, with curtains around them and mattresses piled on top. Over the chimney-piece was a large iron cross, beneath which – and above the blazing fire – was a brightly coloured portrait of the Virgin Mary. In the chimney corner sat an old and rather bent woman, with something on her head that might have been a man's night-cap. From time to time she stood up with some difficulty and turned the pancakes that were frying – and smelling remarkably good, thought William – in a large copper pan.

She may have been surprised to see William, but gave no indication of it, merely grunting: '*M'sieur*' and continuing with her cooking. There followed a long explanation by Lucie, which William could not understand at all, and some cackles of laughter from the old woman, which William found alarming. Then she disappeared behind the curtain to return with the pale, quiet boy, who was no longer so pale, his face being bright in the firelight.

William found himself unable to speak, so convinced was he now that he had not been mistaken and that this child was the son of his best friend, the child whose portrait he had painted six years before, the child who had drowned.

'Azicklezad,' said Lucie triumphantly.

'*Oui. C'est moi*,' said the boy.

'I do not believe you,' said William, finding his tongue suddenly. 'I believe that your real name is Sir Nicholas Tremaine, and that you are from England, and that you were shipwrecked here six years ago.'

'*Comprends pas, M'sieur*,' said the boy.

At which the old lady with much puffing and panting fetched a pottery plate from a distant shelf, returned to the fire, removed a beautiful brown pancake from the pan, and handed it to her visitor. Meanwhile William in some frustration had said:

'Oh, I wish you would *comprend*. You are an English milord.' He stood up straight and made the face of an English milord which merely convulsed the children with laughter. 'You are to return to England with me and live in a, em, a *château*.'

'*Il ne comprend pas, M'sieur*,' said Lucie, and asked him in French to produce some more eggs.

'I think,' said William, tasting the pancake and burning his tongue on it, 'I think you are English. English. *Anglais*.'

Immediately the boy's face lightened and he trotted off to the corner in which the beds were stowed. From under one of them he removed a tattered picture book. He placed this in William's lap with a command that he should read it. William raised the book to catch what little light the room contained and saw the familiar cover and title, *Old Mother Hubbard*. He turned to the title page and found there what he most desired to find; and yet in a curious way feared. There was the inscription in his own hand: 'To the little lad, with best wishes on his fourth birthday, from William Randle'. There could be no doubt. It was a miracle of coincidence, a double miracle, for Nicholas had first been saved from the sea and had now been found.

In a hoarse voice William said: 'I gave you this book myself.'

'*M'sieur?*'

William went down on his knees. It seemed to the old woman that he was praying but he wished to show Nico the words which he had written so long ago. He held the book in front of the boy and traced with his forefinger the words, instructing Nico to repeat them after him:

' "To the little lad," ' said William.

'Azicklezad,' said Nico.

'Yes, of course! "With best wishes on his fourth birthday from William Randle." And that's me.' He stood up, and pointed at his beard. '*I* am William Randle.' The three of them stared at him in friendly incomprehension. The old woman seemed most concerned that he had only eaten half of his pancake. William concluded by saying: 'And I am come to take you home.'

There was a deal of explaining to do, and the priest was brought in by Lucie because he knew, or claimed to know, a few words of English. When William's intentions became clear, there was no end of a scene. The old woman – known to all as Mère Annette – was in despair. He had eaten her pancakes (he had indeed on that fateful night eaten a second and a third) and now he meant to take away her child. By what right? She wrung her hands. Would he be happy in a strange country and amongst strange people? She burst into tears. William offered her money, as much as he could afford and a fortune to her. She refused it, and wept all the harder.

Her grief was no less affecting for being noisy. William felt like a villain in a melodrama, especially when Nicholas clung to Mère Annette's skirts and refused to be parted from her. But parted he was with the help of the priest and a black-haired Breton man who arrived on the scene two days after William's appearance in Mère Annette's house. The Breton was called François Penvraz and he claimed to be Nico's father. But when he heard the story which the bearded Englishman never tired of telling he came round to the idea that his 'son' was in fact an English milord. Since he had none of Mère Annette's scruples about accepting William's money, a deal was soon struck, and, like it or not, the little lad had to go. Mère Annette was a little less wretched when two fine cows arrived at the door; these she accepted with enthusiasm. One cow had been her heart's desire for years; what could she say of two?

As soon as a date for Nico's departure was confirmed, William sent a telegram from the Plougastel post office to Lady Tremaine, and thought with pleasure of the happiness it would bring her. He felt sad too, sad that the simple, happy life the boy had enjoyed amongst these good people was to come to an end. Who could guess how he might fare in England?

The day of the departure was grey and stormy. The entire village, it seemed, had turned out to bid him adieu. To reach the boat Nico had to cross over a narrow and rickety plank. He hesitated. The plank shook. He froze where he stood. William encouraged him to take the first tentative steps, but then he looked down at the sea surging against the harbour wall.

In the swirling water he seemed to see once more the face of his mother, her auburn hair framing her face. No amount of encouragement then could persuade him to move, and William had little choice but to carry him to the ship, followed by his trunk. The last the Plougastel villagers could clearly see of their Azicklezad was his legs kicking wildly as he was hoisted without ceremony into the vessel which would carry him out of their lives. Mère Annette and Lucie were inconsolable. Even François, a sturdy and unemotional fisherman, was seen to brush his eyes with his sleeve more than once.

Chapter Fourteen

Bootle was postmaster and stationmaster and just-about - everything - else - you - can - think - of - master. When he was being a stationmaster, which was not very often, for trains rarely stopped at Trecastle, he wore the uniform of an employee of the Great Western Railway. When he was being a postmaster he wore the uniform of an employee of the General Post Office and when he was being everything-else-you-can-think-of he wore a selection of other uniforms which he had found in a large theatrical hamper, delivered to Trecastle Station but never claimed. So that sometimes Bootle appeared to be a lieutenant in the French Foreign Legion, sometimes a Canadian Mountie, sometimes a Red Indian, and – once a year – Father Christmas.

He was dressed as a postmaster when he pulled at the bell of the Dower House so fiercely that it seemed likely he would bring the bell down and the Dower House with it.

'Dulcie! Dulcie!' he cried.

Dulcie appeared adjusting her cap. 'I am not to disturb Her Ladyship before nine o'clock under any circumstances. Not for Her Majesty herself, I wouldn't.' In Dulcie's mind she imagined Her Majesty riding up to the Dower House in the Coronation Coach, and demanding to be admitted. And she, Dulcie, curtseying most politely and saying: I'm *so* sorry, Your Majesty, but do call back in half an hour. 'More than my job's worth,' she concluded.

'I think you may, Dulcie, all the same.'

Dulcie sniffed. Who did Bootle think he was? 'I will thank you to keep your Dulcies to yourself,' she said and sniffed, the first sniff having made her want to sniff again. But then curiosity impelled her to add: 'And what is so important that I must wake Her Ladyship?'

'I have this telegram for her.' He showed her the official-looking, yellow envelope.

'And what does it say?'

'You know I may not tell you that.' Quickly Bootle added: 'That is to say, I don't know what it contains.'

'In that case how do you know it is important enough to dusturb my mistress?'

Bootle felt sure that there ought to be an answer to this but he could not for the life of him think of one.

'What if it needs an answer?' he asked.

Dulcie grabbed the telegram from him.

'If it needs an answer,' she said pertly, 'it shall have an answer, when my mistress is ready to give you one.'

And with that she shut the door in his face, conscious of having done her duty, and preserved her dignity.

Now Bootle had a real dilemma. Officially he did not know what was in the telegram. He had told Dulcie that he did not. But as he waited outside the Dower House he was joined by several others from the village, and they demanded to know the news. He told them he could not answer their questions, and they refused to believe him. He persisted and they sneered at him. And all the time he was burning to tell them because what can be pleasanter than giving good news to people you are fond of?

Dulcie brought her mistress the telegram on the breakfast tray. Lady Tremaine cut the top off her soft-boiled egg and began to eat the flesh with her silver spoon. Dulcie coughed quietly to draw attention to the telegram.

'Do you have a cough, Dulcie?' Lady Tremaine sternly inquired. After this there was nothing for it but to wait until breakfast was over. Then and only then was the envelope opened with a paper-knife which Dulcie had to fetch from downstairs.

Not until she read it, did Lady Tremaine show any emotion, but she more than made up for her earlier restraint. She flung back the bedclothes, sending the tray flying, and let loose a yell of pure happiness.

'It's Nicholas!' she cried. 'He's alive!' And with that she embraced her maid and danced her round the room, an event which Dulcie would not have believed possible. Then it was Dulcie's turn, having flung the window wide, to shout to the assembled villagers:

'It's Sir Nicholas! He's alive!'

Then the village of Trecastle cheered. It threw its arms into the air. It rang its bells. It was as though it had been asleep for a hundred years and had just been kissed by a handsome prince.

The details became known. The Tremaine heir was on his way to Trecastle; he was travelling with that nice William Randle who had found him in Brittany. He would arrive that very afternoon. It was exactly six years since he had been expected and feared drowned.

'If only his grandfather had lived to see this day,' said Lady Tremaine.

It was not long before Dulcie asked the question to which everyone wished to hear the answer: what was now going to be the fate of Sir – or rather Master – Gerald?

Chapter Fifteen

Gerald was at breakfast with his mother and sister when the bells began to peal. He had been complaining to Robinson that Cook had cut the rind off the bacon rashers. That was not the way bacon was eaten in London. In future, he added, he would like his bacon cut thin and with the rinds on and crispier. Then came the bells which put all such thoughts quite out of his mind.

Joanna asked why the bells were being rung, and Robinson said that he did not know but would go and find out. While he did so, Margaret said that she thought it was a wonderfully happy sound. And by the time Robinson returned, Gerald had guessed the truth.

'Nicholas has been found?'

'Why, yes, Master Gerald, yes.'

'Master Gerald,' said Joanna, 'then he is no longer a baronet.' She gave a low moan, and stumbled from the room. Margaret followed her.

'But Mother,' she said, 'this is wonderful news.'

Joanna looked at her daughter as though she was a complete stranger. 'Wonderful news? Are you out of your mind, Margaret? Wonderful news? Everything we have, everything we *are* is being taken from us. You call that wonderful news?'

'A boy who was believed drowned is safe and well. That is wonderful, surely.'

Joanna's face was closed, like a fist. 'But what about us?' she said.

As for Robinson, eighty years of not showing what he was feeling had not stopped him having feelings. Indeed his feelings were possibly more passionate than those of someone who shouts and laughs and weeps in public. Later he was to explain to his friends in the public house that the unexpected news of Sir Nicholas's homecoming had nearly proved fatal to him.

'Had it not been for the occasional dose of peppermint water, which is the finest medicine of all, I would have surely died of combustion of the heart.'

About midday Lady Tremaine was shown by Robinson into the library of her former home. Not without difficulty she took down the heavy family Bible and placed it on a brass lectern. Then she opened it at the front page which was handsomely decorated with flowers and tree fronds and women leaning on bits of statues. It also depicted over several pages the long and distinguished history of the Tremaine family, ending with the latest entry:

Nicholas Tremaine, a little lad who would have been a sailor had God spared his life. Born 1875. Died 1880.

Taking up a pen, Lady Tremaine struck out this entry and added the following:

The sea has given up her dead, and our boy is come home.

Margaret came in and stood nervously by the door, waiting for the old lady to look up and acknowledge her presence. When she did so, Margaret said:

'I am so happy for you, Lady Tremaine.'

'Thank you, my dear.'

'It seems like a miracle.'

'How kind you are. I rather hoped that your mother . . .'

'She sent me to say that she has been taken poorly, and asks to be forgiven.'

Margaret was not a natural liar, and telling other people's lies is even harder than telling one's own. Lady Tremaine had lived long enough to understand this, however. Gently she said:

'How may I make it easier for her?'

Just then the heavy doors of the library swung open, and there was Joanna, ready to speak for herself.

'I have been considering the rumours in the village,' she said, 'and it seems clear to me, Lady Tremaine, that we are the victims of a heartless joke.'

Lady Tremaine held out the telegram to her.

'I have the telegram, Mrs Tremaine. It is clear and unambiguous. William Randle says that there can be no possible doubt. He has found my grandson, Nicholas, and is bringing him home.'

'William Randle!' And she grabbed the telegram. 'I knew his hand would be in this. He has acted deliberately – from spite.'

Margaret's sense of justice was outraged by this, and she interrupted her mother to protest. Her reward was to be ordered to her room immediately.

'But why? What have I done?'

'Do you suppose that you are unaffected by all this?

79

How wrong you are, my dear! You might have had any young man in the county, and now we will all be a laughing stock.' She snapped her fingers in the air, as if to show how lightly people would dismiss them when they found that they were no longer the heirs to the Tremaine name and the Trecastle estates.

'But, Mother, I am *pleased*.'

Lady Tremaine looked from mother to daughter, the one so full of bitterness, the other so innocent. She wondered how it came about that such a mother could have such a daughter, and it led her to thinking about her own son, Walter, and how proud she had been of him, and of the awful day on which she had learned of his death by drowning. But now perhaps through *his* son she might recapture some of that pride of motherhood. And thinking of her son and of her son's son led her to thinking of Joanna's son, who had been so willing to call her Grandmama.

'Where is Gerald?' she asked.

*   *   *

When the weather was fine Lady Tremaine occasionally took a stroll along the cliffs. That afternoon she came across Gerald sitting close to the edge, his arms around his knees, and Dandy beside him, cropping grass. Lady Tremaine stood for a while behind him, leaning on her silver-handled stick, looking where he was looking, out across the sea.

Gently, Lady Tremaine said at last: 'The sea gives up its dead.'

'Do you suppose he remembers this place?'

'He was very young when he left it.'

Turning to look up at her, Gerald asked: 'What should I call you now, Grandmama?'

'Why, Grandmama still, I hope.'

'And shall we meet, Nicholas and I?'

'Of course you shall, and be good friends. Why ever not?'

Gerald stood, and Dandy thrust his soft muzzle into the boy's chest.

'Mama says that we may have to return to London.'

'Would you wish it?'

''Course not, Grandmama. You can't fly kites in London.'

Smelling the salty air and hearing the raucous gulls, and leaning slightly into the breeze which blew always from the sea, Lady Tremaine said:

'Just because you are no longer a baronet does not mean that you are no longer a Tremaine. And the Tremaines belong in Trecastle. They always have and they always will.'

'I'm glad.'

'You're a good boy, Gerald.'

Gerald looked deep into her eyes, and said with an earnestness she found touching: 'No, I am not. For when I heard the news, I wished him still to be dead. But now, Grandmama, I am happy that you are happy.' He put his hand on her arm. 'Will you love him more than me?'

By way of reply she clasped him tightly to her. He smelt the scent of lavender and then, breaking away from her, he shouted out across the sea as loudly as he possibly could and with a mounting and alarming excitement:

'Nicholas! Nicholas!'

*   *   *

Thirty miles out to sea Nicholas sat huddled on the deck of the steamship, his face in his hands, his fingers in his ears, his eyes tight shut, rocking himself gently to and fro.

Leaning against the rail William Randle, believing the boy to be at his side, pointed across the sea to the faintest smudge of grey on the horizon.

'There!' he said with pride. 'That is the coast of Cornwall.' Receiving no answer and seeing no child next to him, he went in search of his charge, and found him still rocking and still hunched in a tight bundle of terror.

'Why, there you are, old chap,' said Randle, 'are you all right? Not sea-sick or anything?'

Since Nicholas could neither see nor hear him, no answer was forthcoming. But sea-sick he certainly was.

*　　　*　　　*

As Gerald led Dandy back through the village he was watched by a knot of curious children. A few of them might have felt sorry for him, but most felt that he had deserved what had befallen him. Tom Austen and his sister, Peggy, were standing with Joe Snell, and as Gerald, looking neither to right nor left, approached, Tom whipped off his jacket and laid it down in the road in front of him, saying:

'Hello, Dutchie.'

'Who's a baronite now?' jeered Joe Snell.

'You be one of us now,' said Tom.

'Nah!' cried Joe. 'He's nothing. Not dirt beneath Sir Nicholas's heel.'

'Maybe,' cried Peggy to Gerald, seeing which way the wind was blowing, 'maybe he'll take you on as his stable boy.'

As Gerald stepped on Tom's jacket, Joe took hold of an edge of it and whipped it away, sending Gerald flying into the mud. He picked himself up and continued his journey, leading the pony and ignoring the jeers. But then suddenly he spun round on his heels and delivered a terrific blow to the point of Joe's jaw. It was most impressive. There was a respectful silence as Joe picked himself up and considered what to do for the best. Then to everybody's surprise – perhaps even to Joe's – he nodded to Gerald and, putting his arm around the boy's back, walked off with him. It was Peggy Austen, jaw cocked, eyes merciless, who said what the others were thinking:

'Turncoat! Can't depend on no one these days. Least of all the bloomin' Dutch.'

But Peggy's brother was more charitable: 'Poor Master Gerald, I'd not be in your boots for a gold clock.'

Chapter Sixteen

Lady Tremaine was anxious to clarify the complicated situation that had arisen since the arrival of Randle's telegram, and entered at once into correspondence by telegram with Mr Apted of Lincoln's Inn. She discovered that she was the natural guardian of Sir Nicholas and that, until he was twenty-one, she would be in total control of the management of his estate and fortunes. She was entitled to live in the Dower House, and to receive a modest annual allowance.

Joanna Tremaine, Margaret and Gerald had no claims at all on the estate.

She inquired whether it would be possible to settle some money upon her kinspeople, a thousand a year, say, on Gerald, and five hundred a year, say, on Joanna and Margaret and, in return, require them to live in the big house and provide for the upkeep of the place and the feeding and education of Sir Nicholas.

Mr Apted advised that such an arrangement was perfectly legal, but far too generous.

Lady Tremaine snorted as she relayed Mr Apted's views to Robinson. 'If it were left to the generosity of such as Mr Apted, no doubt we should all be standing at the kerbside begging for bread!'

And when this proposal was conveyed to Joanna, she too regarded it with disfavour. 'So, I am to be head nursery-maid!' she explained to Margaret. 'As to what Gerald and you are to be, the Lord knows!'

Margaret had hoped that she would be able to tell Lady Tremaine that they were all delighted with the arrangement, but Joanna's instructions were rather different:

'You are certainly to convey to her how grateful we are. You may add how humble we are, how deeply indebted we are, and how if she asked us to eat dirt we would graciously obey her every command.' But then her expression changed. 'You may also tell her that we shall need persuasive evidence before we accept that this upstart is who he claims to be.'

'Is there any doubt, Mother?' Margaret asked.

'When you have seen as much of the wickedness of the world as I have, you too will become sceptical. Is it unreasonable to ask for proof?'

*　　　*　　　*

Those who had been present at the previous occasion on which the village had gathered to welcome the Tremaine heir to Trecastle could not avoid noticing the contrast. Then there had been no triumphal arch, no town band, no cheering and clapping, and Gerald, Joanna and Margaret had rattled through the streets unheralded and unsung.

They would also recall how an earlier welcome had been ruined by a cruel fate, how the cheers had frozen on the lips, and the bells remained unrung, how the rain had lashed down on the triumphal arch, and how no young Nicholas, no Walter and no Elizabeth had appeared to charm and delight the adoring inhabitants.

There would be no gallant Captain Walter now, no gracious Elizabeth Tremaine, but never mind. The young baronet had returned as though by a miracle from the grave. In the church, the Reverend Clowes said a special prayer of thanksgiving, and in the pub for this one day the beer was free.

The welcome began at Trecastle Station. William Randle stepped first from the steaming train; he was closely followed by Nicholas in an overcoat bought for him at Cherbourg. Nicholas stood blinking on the platform, alarmed by the band's rendition of 'See the Conquering Hero Comes' and bewildered by the cheering. Clearly something was expected of him, but he had no notion what.

Bootle, wearing his Great Western Railway uniform, from which he had painstakingly removed the gravy stains, cleared his throat loudly. Someone had to say something, and he was the official.

'Ladies and gentlemen . . .' he announced. The train-driver chose that moment to release the brake, and as the train moved off with a whistle and a couple of puffs, steam appeared from between Bootle's legs. He tried again. 'Ladies and gentlemen . . .'

'Get on with it!' shouted the villagers.

'It has fallen to me, reluctant as I am, to be the first to welcome Sir Nicholas back to the home of his ancestors.'

'You'll frighten him off again!' came the cry and much

raucous laughter.

Bootle was unnerved. He glanced into the palm of his hand for the notes he had concealed there, but the steam had got to them and the ink had run. He smiled desperately for inspiration but none was forthcoming.

'So I er . . .' he said, and launched into a prolonged coughing fit, but that failed to help either, 'so I er . . . I do. I bid you welcome.'

William Randle held up his hands for silence, and said:

'Sir Nicholas does not speak English, and the Lord knows I do not speak French, but I am sure I speak for both of us when I say how sincerely glad we both are to be home.'

The procession through the village was very touching. The white goose cackled and the grey donkey brayed, and somebody had hung around Peterkin's neck a large piece of cardboard on which was inscribed very finely in red and blue and gold crayon:

WELCOME TO MY NOBLE LITTLE RIDER.

(The sign did not stay there long. Peterkin bucked and plunged and kicked and reared until it was dislodged.) Bunting was hung from many windows, and the bell-ringers rolled up their sleeves and pealed with all their might. Nicholas saw the bunting and the villagers. He heard the church bells and the cheering and the music. But it was not until he saw his own old pony that somewhere in his brain a connection was made. 'Peterkin,' he murmured in a voice full of wonder, adding: *Je crois que je me souviens . . .*

At the big house there was a notable reception. The servants, from the smallest hall-boy to the awe-inspiring

Robinson, were lined up on the granite steps. To the left stood Lady Tremaine and Dulcie; to the right the 'new' family, Joanna and Margaret and Gerald. It was expected that there might have been angry words exchanged between the two kinswomen, but sparks did not fly. Joanna merely remarked in a mild enough tone:

'I thought you might have gone to the station.'

To which Lady Tremaine responded: 'This is his house and these are his people. I think this is where my duty lies.'

These two simple sentences struck at the very heart of Joanna's anguish. She said nothing further but grabbed her dispossessed son and held him very tight in front of her.

When the old carriage carrying William Randle and Nicholas drew up in front of the big house, two footmen stepped forward to open the doors. As Nicholas climbed out he looked very tiny in his fine big overcoat. Standing on the driveway with the big house in front of him and family, friends and servants on all sides, he hesitated a moment, then walked boldly forward to the extreme left of the group of well-wishers. Moving along the group he bowed slightly to each in turn, saying as he did so in his stilted English:

''Ow do you do? 'Ow do you do? 'Ow do you do?'

When he reached old Robinson, the butler shook him firmly by the hand and said in his cracked, old voice:

'Welcome home, Sir Nicholas, I little thought I should live to see the day.'

And when he reached his grandmother, the tall, graceful and dignified woman, as unlike his other grandmother, Mère Annette, as it was possible to be, she took him in her arms and embraced him:

'Nico, oh Nico,' she said. 'I thank God that you have returned to us.'

Wriggling out of her arms, Nico said: ' 'Ow do you do, Madame?'

'No, my darling, Grandmama, not Madame.'

But Nicholas was too confused, too dispirited, too tired after the long journey and the conflicting emotions, to understand what was required of him. Lady Tremaine was left feeling that this small, undeveloped, seemingly unhelpful little creature was a sad disappointment.

It was Gerald who suggested that he take Nicholas off to see Peterkin. At the familiar name Nicholas perked up and trotted off happily enough with his cousin, while Margaret issued an invitation to Lady Tremaine and William Randle that they should both dine at the big house that night. Although the invitation was supposedly from Joanna, it had in fact been Margaret's idea, and the kitchen staff had been hard at work all day preparing a meal fit for an occasion as festive as this one. Before the company dispersed, Joanna was overheard by some of these servants to remark to her daughter:

'Frankly, Margaret, I was curious to see what sort of an urchin William would have drummed up to play the part of Sir Nicholas Tremaine. What did you think? Not very convincing in my view. Not convincing at all.'

The Trecastle stables were as old as the house. Clustering around a paddock, they were built of pink brick – rare in Cornwall – and wistaria climbed around their leaded windows. Baker, the groom, was responsible for the well-being of the coach-horses, the hunters and the ponies, and from time to time he enlisted the help of Joe Snell and Tom Austen to turn the straw bedding or replenish the hay troughs or polish the tackle or muck out the stalls. It was to the stables that Gerald brought Nicholas, and there they found Peterkin, saddled and bridled, ears pricked as though he too realised that this was a rather special occasion.

As soon as Nico saw Peterkin, he pushed forward and buried his face in the pony's neck.

'Ride him,' said Gerald, and, in case the boy did not understand, Tom offered him a leg up. Once in the saddle, Nico seemed nervous and ill at ease, and walked the pony slowly around the field.

'Peterkin waited six years for that?' was Joe's sarcastic comment, and Gerald muttered:

'If that's the best he can do, I don't see why he can't have just any old pony.'

'Maybe they go slower in France,' said Tom.

When Nico brought Peterkin back to base, Joe said:

'At least give 'im a trot,' and landed such a slap on the pony's rump with a riding crop that Peterkin took off as though all the hounds of Hell were after him. Nicholas, taken by surprise, was caught off balance, and, with his feet out of the irons, it was all he could do to stay in the saddle. He leant forward and put one arm around the pony's neck while clutching the mane with his free hand.

Unused to such exertions, Peterkin completed one circuit of the field and returned to the stables. Gerald commented that Nico was clearly not much of a horseman, but Tom, impressed that the lad had at least clung on, remarked that he would surely do better when he was used to it. This was true. Nico was a very fair rider back in Brittany, but there he rode bare-back.

'Come on, Nico,' said Gerald. 'It's clear you can handle Peterkin, so I'll show you the harbour.'

The masts of the fishing boats had been bedecked with flags and they made a cheerful display as they bobbed in the choppy seas secure within the protection of the harbour walls. Several of the fishermen, having welcomed Sir Nicholas back to the village, were filling in that awkward couple of hours between the after-lunch snooze and the early evening opening of the pub by playing crib on the jetty, when the two boys appeared. Gerald headed for the slipway.

'Come on, Nico,' he cried, 'we can go for a row round the bay.'

Nicholas held back. '*Non. Je n'veux pas,*' he said.

Gerald shrugged. 'It's only salt water,' and he set off briskly down the slipway which was slimy with the scales of pilchards. 'If you want to go home, Nicholas, it's that way,' and he waved an airy hand in the general direction of the big house.

Nicholas climbed the hill through the village and tried to pretend that he was not aware of the faces watching him from behind lace curtains. Reaching the village green, he spent a few minutes with the animals tethered there, the old donkey and the goat, and then he crouched down and talked to the ducks, the chickens and the geese. The animals did not mind that he talked to them in French.

Chapter Seventeen

In those days dinners really were dinners. Although there might only be two courses, each course consisted of a dozen or more dishes, served all at once, so that soup, meat and fish, jellies and puddings would all be placed on the table at the same time; then the table would be re-laid, and another selection of dishes put before the (rather less hungry) guests. Lady Tremaine had maintained the highest standards. Her cook had learned her business in one of the best houses in London, working to a French chef, who was meticulous in every particular. Although unused to entertaining – Lady Tremaine had dined alone for so many years – the cook had not lost her skills. Lady Tremaine liked plain food, but the finest quality. She ate sparingly and enjoyed what she ate.

But Joanna had demanded changes of the cook. Hot food was to be served directly from the kitchen and handed round to the guests by the footmen. She favoured grand set pieces made out of sugar and aspic, and a dinner party such as the one to welcome Nicholas home was an opportunity to be very grand, or, as she explained to Robinson, to 'push the boat out'. So there was ox-tongue and sirloin of beef, there was roast goose and fricandeau of veal, there were oysters and lobsters, and vegetables in profusion. To follow there were fairy fancies and jelly tartlets served with clotted cream, and quince custard and lemon cheese.

The children, unused to such luxury, ate far too much of the early dishes, and could do little more than sit and stare at what followed. By the time the potted cheeses were handed round, there were few takers.

What everyone wished to hear was William's story of how he came to find Azicklezad, and he told the story simply at first and later with embellishments. When William first mentioned Lucie, Nicholas looked up sharply and asked:

'Lucie? Où est-elle?'

But nobody heard him. A little later he helped himself to a leg of goose and, holding it in his right hand, began gnawing at it. Lady Tremaine shouted at him to behave himself and frightened him so much that he ran out of the room and sat on the stairs, wondering what it was that he had done wrong and in what way he had upset the grand old lady. Robinson came after him and tried to comfort him, telling him that there was never a child more welcome to Trecastle than he was, 'no, not since the baby that was born in a manger', and, although Nicholas did not understand a word the butler was saying, he found comfort in the old man's voice and allowed himself to be led back into the great dining room.

A while later, in an attempt to lighten the party, Randle

announced a toast: 'To Little Sir Nicholas, with our heart-felt affection and gratitude to God for his safe return.' Everyone stood and raised their glasses and smiled and turned to Sir Nicholas only to find that the boy had fallen fast asleep and was snoring gently, as he dreamed of his home in Plougastel, and of playing on the beach with Lucie and his many friends.

As Dulcie accompanied Lady Tremaine home across the park, there was a strong breeze from the sea and clouds scudded across the face of the moon. Distantly could be heard the sound of the waves crashing on the rocks as the tide thrust itself into secret caves and churned up silent rock-pools into whirlpools of phosphorescent foam.

'Frankly,' said Lady Tremaine, 'I was disappointed in the child.'

'He must have been tired after his journey, milady.'

'Well yes, of course, and our ways must seem very strange to him. Nonetheless I should have been better pleased to have observed something of Master Gerald's liveliness in his face.'

'The poor wee lamb,' said Dulcie who, never having had children herself, thought them all sweet and charming little creatures.

'Poor wee lambs are all very fine, Dulcie, but not if they are destined to serve in the Royal Navy.'

Meanwhile in the library of the big house, Joanna was alone with William. Open on her lap was *Old Mother Hubbard*. She spoke gently to the handsome young man, but her questions were barbed.

'This book was by the boy's bed? There can be no doubt of that?'

'None.'

'And it was the very same book which you had given him

all those years before?'

'The inscription is in my hand. You may see for yourself, Mrs Tremaine.'

'And you would swear to that?'

'In any court of law.'

'I remain unconvinced.'

But then Randle spoke of the trunk of belongings which had come from the wreck, and reminded Joanna that the boy had recognised Peterkin, his old pony.

'But there is proof positive, Mrs Tremaine. I painted his portrait. I cannot be mistaken.'

That night Nicholas dreamt that he was back on the *Alberta*. He saw the mountainous, green waves, and heard the cry of the helmsman as the lightning bolt shattered the rigging. There was his father shouting to him as the decks tilted and the thunder rumbled, and there was his mother, her hair around her beautiful face, as she slipped beneath the sea. And he reached out to her but his arms were not long enough, and he swam towards her but his strokes were not strong enough, and he lost her for ever, and he would never see her again . . .

'Nicholas! Nicholas!' cried Margaret. She was sitting above him in her white nightgown and shaking him awake. 'Wake up! Wake up!' At last he opened his eyes, and stared about him wildly, knowing neither where he was, nor who this girl was. She seemed to be trying to talk to him in a sort of French, but he could make no sense of this at all. She was clearly mad and, as soon as the memory of the nightmare had begun to fade, he told her so.

This she understood, but seemed not to mind. And she insisted on bathing his fevered brow with a damp towel and straightening out his crumpled sheets and staying with him until he slept – quite peacefully this time.

Morning came. The sky was the palest of pinks behind the silhouette of the big house which appeared to have no dimensions, like a cut-out. Nicholas awoke early and looked out of the window. A cock crowed. In the distance he could just make out the old donkey shifting its legs on the village green. His friend!

With great care he eased open the heavy mahogany door of his bedroom and pattered down the grand staircase past his dignified ancestors in their gilded frames. The stone flags of the hall were cold under his bare feet. There was a clang as he raised the latch and a creak as he pushed against the front door, but he was soon out of the house and down the driveway.

An hour later Gerald burst into his mother's bedroom.

'Quickly, Mother, quickly!' he cried as he shook her awake. 'You've got to see this.'

Joanna was most displeased. She had been dreaming of being presented at St James's Palace, and it was her turn next. 'Gerald, what on earth is the matter? Have you taken leave of your senses?'

'Not I!' he cried. 'Do come.'

Joanna had little choice, for Gerald was tugging at her arm, like a terrier at a tree-root. The two of them joined an assembly of servants, who were huddled chattering at the entrance to the library. As Joanna approached they fell silent and parted to let her through.

The window to the terrace had been opened, and all the animals from the village had been invited in. On the rug were two pigs, one white and one black, with impressive curly tails. There were cocks and hens pecking at the Turkish carpet. Joanna found herself face to face with a large and amiable-looking cow. Nicholas was grinning broadly and talking to his varied guests in a torrent of

French. As soon as he saw Joanna, he turned to her and spread his arms in pride:

'*Mes amis*,' he cried, 'my friends!'

But his happy expression turned to one of anxiety and bewilderment as he registered the cold and contemptuous horror on the face of Joanna. She hated him. She was implacable. He remained where he was, his arms outspread, but the smile faded from his lips.

Chapter Eighteen

The autumn months that followed Sir Nicholas's return to his ancestral home were amongst the stormiest that the sailors on that wild Cornish coast could remember. It seemed as though the wind was always howling, the sea always raging. And try as he might to conquer his fears there was scarcely a night when he did not huddle in bed with his hands over his ears, trying to drown out those sounds which he still associated with the death of his beloved parents.

Frequently Margaret came to his room and tried to reassure him. She would teach him English, a few words at a time, and explain to him about the Tremaines, and how they had always been good sailors, and why his grandmother was disappointed that he seemed so little interested in the sea and so anxious to stay well away from it.

Gerald had his anxieties too, which he shared with Margaret.

'What will happen when we get older? Will Nico send us back to London?'

'Why should he?'

'Why should he not?'

'Should you like to go back?'

'Not I. I mean never to be parted from the sea again.'

'Do you remember our big house in London when Father was still alive?'

'Tell me about it. Was it as big as this?'

'Of course not, but it was big for London. The ceilings were high but sometimes Father would lift me on his shoulders to see if I could touch them, but I never could. And when he let me down I left my stomach behind.'

'Tell me more, Margaret.'

'Sometimes I could hear Mama singing as she went about the house.'

'I don't remember that either.'

One frosty morning, when for a change the wind was just a gentle breeze, Gerald and Margaret went to Mr Penfold's shop to collect some pearl buttons which Joanna had ordered from Penzance. Meticulously neat, the shop contained lemonade powder and bootlaces, mouse-traps and cut-glass bowls, leggings and lampshades. Mr Penfold promised his customers that if he could not find an item within thirty seconds, he would reduce the price of that item by half. Old Mr Penfold, whose weatherbeaten face and peg-leg testified to a career at sea, was intent upon carving some fine details on a model of a frigate in full sail. Gerald gasped when he saw it.

'That's a handsome boat,' he cried.

'Aye. Correct in each pertickler.'

'Where will you sail her, Penfold? Can I come and watch?'

'Why, bless you, she bain't for me.'

'Whose is she then?'

'Well, she be for young Sir Nicholas. Only I have not quite finished her, and Lady Tremaine means me to have her ready in time for Christmas.'

Gerald muttered something bitterly to Margaret, but Mr Penfold, whose hearing was sharper than his other faculties, explained:

'Ah well, you see, there's a story attached to this ship. Captain Walter, that's Sir Nicholas's father, asked me to carve her for the boy for his birthday. So I set to with a will. But then of course I put her aside when the lad was drownded, and picked her up again when he wasn't drownded no more. So now he is to have the ship after all. For his father's sake, and his own.'

Margaret examined the model more closely. Everything was perfectly to scale, and even the knots in the rigging and the plates on the Captain's table were marvellously authentic. Masts, sails and cannon all seemed to have come out of Her Majesty's dockyard. Margaret voiced her admiration, and Penfold was hard put to it to conceal his pleasure.

'Well, you see, Miss, she's modelled on a frigate I served on when I was ship's carpenter.'

Gerald's eyes blazed. 'Did you see action, Penfold?'

'Did I not!' He came out from behind the counter and tapped his wooden leg. 'Where do you think this went, eh? Well, I'll tell 'ee. I left it behind on the deck of the *Furious* after we'd been fired on by the battery at Odessa. A cannon ball took it clean off and there I was, hopping a hornpipe and yelling blue murder till they held me down. And the sawbones took it off at the knee and sealed the end with pitch, and all the while they were pouring grog down me.

And just as they finished I could hear them cheering for the victory, and I even raised a bit of a cheer meself.'

During this recital Margaret and Gerald had turned quite pale.

'Nay, but what do a leg signify? It were a great victory, and I were there.'

'I mean to be an admiral one day,' said Gerald.

'Do you indeed? Well, first you will need to be a sailor and a good one, for it's them as does the heavy work. Admiral comes later, when all you're good for is wearing fine clothes.'

'When she's done, can I sail her? Before Sir Nicholas gets her, I mean. Just once would be enough.'

'Indeed you cannot.'

'Then I wish they'd shot off your other leg too,' said Gerald, and stormed out of the shop, leaving Margaret to do the apologising, for which she had quite a talent after so much practice.

The bitterness which Gerald felt was focused on Nicholas. That he and only he should be allowed to ride Peterkin was bad enough; that he and only he should be allowed the pride of ownership and the pleasure of sailing this finest of toys was worse; and that he, who feared and hated the sea, should be regarded as a suitable heir to the Tremaines who loved and honoured it, was insufferable. It was quite unjust. If there was to be any justice for him in the future, Gerald reckoned that it could only come through Lady Tremaine, who appreciated his qualities. He would have to be especially nice to the old lady, and then maybe she would champion him against Little Sir Nicholas, the horseman who seemed scared to break into a trot, the admiral-to-be who feared the sea, the future owner of the big house, who could scarcely string together a decent sentence in English.

Gerald mentioned the matter of Penfold's model ship to his mother, and, although Joanna agreed that there was no reason why Gerald should not be given the ship, it was really none of her business. She said, however, that she would speak to Lady Tremaine when a suitable occasion presented itself.

Margaret was as unhappy as Gerald but in quite a different way. She loved the house and the park, she gloried in the sight and sound of the sea and the freshness of the air, but she was lonely. She could talk to Gerald, but she seemed to be forever scolding him and she hated to be always telling him how to behave. She could talk to her mother, but her mother only wanted to discuss her own problems. She could write to Nolan, and did so frequently, because in these letters she could pour out her true feelings as she could to no one else. But letters were no substitute for friendship.

She thought a good deal about William Randle. He had taken to making sketches of her, and had told her that he was planning a life-size portrait in oils. He confused her. At times it seemed as though he was flattering her, talking to her as if she were fully adult; at other times he ignored her, and she was left irritable and restless. She enjoyed looking at him, and would have liked to be able to sketch him rather than the other way around, for she would not have been so embarrassed. She had shown quite a talent for art during her brief London schooldays.

Joanna was probably jealous of her for, although William Randle had promised to paint a picture of Joanna, when the matter was raised William always seemed to find some excuse to postpone the sitting. One day in William's hearing Joanna told her daughter that she was making arrangements for Margaret to go to an Academy for Young Ladies in London.

In the end it was Randle who broached the matter of the model ship with Lady Tremaine, after Joanna had requested him to.

'You see, William,' Lady Tremaine said over a cup of tea and a shortcake biscuit, 'Walter always adored the sea, and wanted nothing more than that his son should love it as he did.'

'But surely, Lady Tremaine, what Walter would have most wanted would have been the boy's happiness. If Nicholas is given the ship it concerns me that he may feel under great pressure to do what is not natural for him; to pretend to love what he hates. For he does hate the sea. I have seen him cowering and shivering.'

'Oh, stuff and nonsense. He'll get over that. The sea is in his blood.'

'Maybe it was, but he watched his parents drown and was cast adrift for heaven knows how long with no hope of salvation.'

While the old lady sipped her tea she considered seriously what William had said. Her love and admiration for Gerald had increased the longer she had known him, but try as she might she could find little love in her heart for her true grandson. She asked William what he suggested.

'Why not find something the boy would really like? A castle perhaps, or a coach and horses? I could find one in town.'

Lady Tremaine reluctantly agreed to this sensible plan, but added that it was essential that Penfold be warned. If he believed that he had been making the ship for Nicholas and saw it given to Gerald instead he might be difficult and make a scene. She would pay him a visit.

Chapter Nineteen

In the paddock Gerald and Nicholas were racing their ponies, watched by Baker, the groom, and Joe Snell. Joe had offered odds against Nicholas and Peterkin, but Baker had seen Sir Nicholas riding out in the early mornings and had been impressed. He accepted the odds Joe offered.

The race was two circuits of the paddock. After the first Gerald and Dandy were comfortably ahead; after the second Nico had overtaken them on Peterkin and forged clear.

Gerald was ungracious in defeat. 'I'd have beaten you hollow if I'd had the better pony,' was his comment, and then he suddenly spurred Dandy on, and, shouting: 'First to the harbour,' took a healthy lead. The boys raced past Lady Tremaine and Dulcie on their way to Penfold's shop.

'My gracious!' exclaimed Lady Tremaine. 'Cossacks! And who was in the lead, Dulcie? I fancy it was Gerald.' Dulcie had to agree, though she added that in her opinion

Sir Nicholas looked very fine on a pony. Lady Tremaine grunted, and changed the subject: 'I thought I might have a little party this Christmas, my first in the Dower House. Just staff and family and one or two from the village.'

Dulcie said nothing.

'Well, Dulcie?'

'And Mrs Tremaine?'

The two women looked at each other glumly.

Down at the harbour the boys dismounted. On the steeply sloping shingle, fishing boats had been hauled up for tarring and general refurbishments. Some Trecastle fishermen were idly mending nets and gossiping about monstrous fish that they had trawled out of the sea. Nicholas ran forward and joined them.

'May I?' he asked the first fisherman he came to. 'Please?' And he reached out for the net and the hook and thread, which the surprised fisherman was glad to hand to him. The others gathered around and were amazed to see the skill with which Nico set to work.

'Well, I'll be jiggered!' said the fisherman upon whose net Nicholas was at work. 'Would you believe it, lads? A baronet who knows how to mend nets . . . Whatever next?'

'Tell you what, lads,' said a burly red-bearded giant, 'I'm off spinning for mackerel. Will you join me?'

'Yes,' cried an excited Gerald, and added, turning to Nicholas: 'Come on!'

But Nico held back. He was happy mending nets, he said. He could not leave the ponies. It was too cold. The burly fisherman put an arm like a vast leg of mutton on Nicholas's shoulder and guided him towards the boat, but Nicholas pulled back.

'*Non*! *Non*!' And he retreated back up the slipway.

Gerald looked round at the puzzled men, and a cluster of women watching from the jetty.

'It is not important,' he said. 'My cousin is afraid of the sea, that's all. He's a coward, you see.'

The fishermen were bemused. One said he'd be blowed, another that he'd be damned, and a third that he'd be blessed. They then agreed that they never thought they'd live to see the day . . .

*   *   *

Mr Penfold was overcome. Never in all his years in Trecastle had Lady Tremaine honoured his modest premises with her presence. If only she had warned him . . .

But she brushed his apologies aside. It was the ship, she said, that she had come to see. Now that he had finished it, Mr Penfold kept it under a linen cloth. With a touch of the showman he swept the cover aside and displayed his handiwork. Dulcie gasped. Lady Tremaine studied it and asked Mr Penfold to carry it to the window where the light was more favourable. There she studied it more closely. As she did so she murmured:

'I used to be good with my hands. I sewed a patchwork quilt, the stitches so small you could scarcely see them. And each patch unique.' She looked sadly at her hands, twisted now like chickens' claws. 'But your model is magnificent, Mr Penfold, even finer than I had been led to believe.'

'It is all to scale, milady,' said Penfold, almost bursting his buttons with pride, 'even the furniture in the Captain's cabin.'

'I shall be having the Christmas party at the Dower House this year, Mr Penfold, so it will not be quite on the scale of previous years. Nonetheless I am hoping that you will be there, for it is at the Christmas party that I propose to present the ship.'

'Capital, capital, your ladyship! Just to see the little lad's face . . . the image of his father.'

Lady Tremaine glanced at Dulcie before continuing. 'Well, the fact of the matter, Mr Penfold, is this: I am intending to present the ship to Master Gerald. He has quite set his heart on her. And I have observed that Sir Nicholas is not enamoured of the sea.'

'Nicholas not have the ship? Why, Nicholas *must* have the ship! Was it not his father asked me to carve it?'

Dulcie intervened: 'What Lady Tremaine means is . . .'

'Nicholas not have the ship? He's a Tremaine, ain't he?'

'Indeed, it is strange, but . . .'

So great was his indignation that old Penfold rode roughshod over Lady Tremaine's explanation. One thing was clear to him. He had carved the ship for Sir Nicholas, and none but Sir Nicholas should have her.

Meanwhile Lady Tremaine was talking about sending Randle to buy a coach and horses from a toyshop. Toyshop! His ship was no toy.

'I'll tell you what, milady,' he said at length, scratching his head through the greasy cap he always wore, 'let the boy choose. That would be fair. Let him take his pick between this here ship and that there shop-bought toy. Then we'll see.'

'You will be disappointed, I fear, Mr Penfold.'

'Won't be the first time.'

'Very well.'

And so the deal was concluded. And Lady Tremaine left the tiny shop, trailing the scent of lavender, with Dulcie trotting after. Old Penfold snorted and grunted for a while, and muttered to himself about *women* and how they failed to understand the important things in life, and then he lit his pipe and calmed down.

Chapter Twenty

Gerald brought back a dozen fat mackerel, strung together by their gills, from his fishing trip, and very delicious they were, coated in oatmeal and grilled with watercress. Gerald described more than once the skill he had shown in hauling them over the side of the boat, and the determined way he had removed the hooks, before slapping the life out of them against the bottom of the boat.

Later in Nicholas's room, he was unusually friendly.

'It's a shame you're such a coward, Nico,' he said, 'really it is, but I suppose there's nothing to be done about it. It will be my duty to restore the family honour by becoming Admiral of the Fleet.'

'I am not a coward,' muttered Nico, but Gerald carried on regardless.

'Since you like animals, quite the best thing would be for you to become a gentleman farmer. You could manage the estate while I am away at sea. I shall blast the heathen to kingdom come with my fierce cannonfire, and when I return in triumph you will have made Trecastle a place fit for heroes.'

'Why do you call me a coward?'

'Of course Grandmama will be disappointed that it is I, not you, who will be the hero, but I shall comfort her, and I am sure she will be pleased when she sees how beautifully you manage the farm and how sleek and plump the animals are.'

'Why do you say these things? Why do you hate me?'

Gerald turned and looked at his cousin in genuine surprise.

'Hate you? Of course I don't hate you! I feel a little sorry for you, that's all. Goodnight.'

Margaret's room was next to Nicholas's, and she was wakened in the night by the sound of fierce sobbing. Grabbing a shawl she went to him, and found him lying under the bed, his head on a pillow which was soaked through with tears.

'Why, Nico, whatever is the matter?'

'*Je suis un poltron. Gerald m'a dit que je suis un poltron, mais je ne suis pas!*'

This was beyond Margaret's basic French, and all she understood was that Nico was a something-or-other, and that Gerald had called him a something-or-other, and that he wasn't a something-or-other at all. She told Nico to come out from under his bed (which he was pleased to do, since he had become cramped and uncomfortable there), trotted next door to fetch her French dictionary, and returned with the heavy book open at 'p'.

When she discovered that a *poltron* was a coward, she became quite indignant that Gerald should have called Nicholas one.

'You're no coward,' she argued. 'To be afraid of something does not make you a coward! I am afraid of spiders, and not at all keen on black beetles, but that doesn't make me a coward. How can anyone be brave if they do not have fears to overcome? Maybe one day you will quite like the sea.'

'No,' cried Nico, 'I never can.'

Margaret had brought something else from her room, the porcelain Madonna which her father had given her.

'Take this,' she said. 'Keep her by you always. She is from France too. She will give you courage.'

He took the figurine and clutched it to him. At once he felt comforted. The Madonna reminded him of the brightly coloured Madonna above the fireplace at Plougastel. He put his arms around Margaret and she hugged the thin body and put the damp face against her cheek.

'I think,' said Nico in his faltering English, 'I think, Margaret, that maybe you do not 'ate me.'

'Indeed I do not,' she said, 'and why should I? I love you, as we all do.'

After a while she left him, and he fell asleep with the Madonna by his pillow, so that she would be the first thing he would see when he awoke. As for Margaret, she was regretfully aware of the blank space on the wall where the figure used to be. She wondered whether her father would have wanted her to give away the present he had given her; she hoped he would have approved, and on balance she believed he would. To comfort herself as she closed her eyes, she tried to think of Randle's handsome face and to fancy that he had invited her to some grand ball. The only thing was that just as the music started to play and he offered her his arm to lead her on to the floor . . . she fell asleep.

Chapter Twenty-One

As Christmas approached, things went on very quietly in the harbour village of Trecastle. Nico sometimes used to walk by himself to the Dower House and sit with his grandmother and talk to her in his own shy way. Then Gerald would come by, bright and boisterous and affectionate, and, when he appeared, Nicholas fell silent. Lady Tremaine tried to overcome her prejudice against her natural grandson. She heard a story – spread round the village by Tom Austen – about how Gerald had run away from a rather fierce-looking bull while Nicholas had stood his ground and walked past the beast as though walking past a mouse. She was gratified to hear it. (The truth was that the 'bull' was a bullock, which Nico had noticed and Gerald, of course, had not, but then neither had Tom, so that important element did not feature in the retelling of the story.) But she could not pretend, to herself or to those around her, that she preferred Nico to Gerald, and both boys took it to heart.

William Randle completed his oil painting of Margaret and thought it the very best thing he had done. As he modestly told Joanna: 'the *only* good thing I have done'. Joanna was not best pleased. She thought the portrait made Margaret look far too grown up and 'extremely common'. When it was her turn to sit to William, neither of them could pretend that the result was a success.

'I'm sure,' said William tactfully, 'that with a little more work I shall be able to hang it most successfully.'

'I'm sure you will,' Joanna agreed. 'In the Chamber of Horrors.'

Rather than continue to work on a picture so little appreciated, William Randle disappeared, to return a couple of days later with a large and mysterious parcel, impressively wrapped.

Soon afterwards a bulky envelope arrived at the dinner table for Joanna, and she opened it with a glint of triumph in her steely eyes. It was the prospectus of a select and expensive girls' school in London. The following term started in January.

The next day Lady Tremaine received a visit in the library from Mr Apted, very dapper with his Gladstone bag and his gold-rimmed pince-nez. The first contained some settlement papers which Cornelius Strange had drawn up; the second he placed upon his nose in order to read the first.

'These are the papers setting out the annuity you wish Mrs Tremaine and her children to receive from the estate. A thousand pounds for the mother and five hundred each for the children. You are sure you wish to proceed?'

'Quite sure.'

'The sums are exceedingly generous.'

'They are Tremaines, are they not? And Mrs Tremaine

114

bears the brunt of looking after Sir Nicholas.'

From what Apted had heard from Robinson, there was not much 'looking after Sir Nicholas' at all, the boy being left to fend for himself, while Joanna was concerned with making herself beautiful. He considered that Lady Tremaine was acting in haste and that she might well repent at leisure if she and Mrs Tremaine fell out – and there was every reason to suppose that they might.

'Lady Tremaine, might I recommend caution? Why not delay the signing of these papers for a few weeks at least? They cannot, once signed, be unsigned. Wait at least until the new year.'

Lady Tremaine was neither persuaded nor dissuaded. She neither agreed nor disagreed. She kept the papers securely in the family Bible, but did not sign them. Randle accompanied Apted in the train back to London. The artist had the paintings he had done in France with him, and his portrait of Margaret. He also had with him the Joanna portrait, but this he did not intend to take to the Academy. Canvases were expensive, and when he had rented a studio in London, he would paint over the portrait.

Besides Randle's parcel and Apted's papers, other intriguing packages passed through the station at Trecastle as Christmas approached. Nico asked Lady Tremaine if perhaps he could send some Christmas gifts to Mère Annette and Lucie and all his old friends at Plougastel, but to his disappointment Lady Tremaine said that she thought not. It was not healthy, she suggested, to think so much of the past. He ought instead to look ahead. Sadly Nico wondered what there was to look ahead to which might compare with the love and happiness he had enjoyed in Brittany during past Christmases.

Chapter Twenty-Two

The Dower House party took place on Christmas Eve. It was a wintry night with the wind howling in the leafless trees, and the waves beating vindictively against the staunch Cornish cliffs. Even in the security of the small harbour the boats strained and tugged at their moorings. The lighthouse shone out bravely and more than one sailor took comfort from it, checked his position on the charts, and thanked God that he would be home safe and sound for Christmas.

Outside the Dower House, forming two lines either side of the front door and well muffled up against the biting wind, were the servants from the big house, with the Reverend Clowes conducting them in that grand old carol: 'In the Bleak Midwinter'. Lady Tremaine threw open the door; there were the singers and there was Dulcie with a tray of mulled wine for them and mince pies so hot from the oven that you bit into them at your peril. The singers came in and stood round the tree – such a fine tree, not large but perfectly shaped and charmingly decorated by Dulcie – and there they sang two more carols, '*Quelle Est Cette Odeur Agréable?*' in French in honour of Sir Nicholas, and 'Good King Wenceslas', because one could not celebrate Christmas without being reminded of that brave king and his heroic page. Then they drank more toddy, ate more mince pies and were given small but useful gifts, and went to their homes and their families and tried to thaw out.

Back in the Dower House Tom and Peggy Austen played the pipe and fiddle in a piece which they had been practising for weeks. They had played it perfectly when they were alone together, but now in front of an audience 'The Harmonious Blacksmith' sounded quite inharmonious. Tom apologised and Peggy blushed, but everyone said how nicely they had played and how fresh and interesting it had sounded.

Shortly afterwards Joanna arrived with Margaret and Gerald and Nico. They were just in time for the high-spot of this and every Christmas, Robinson's recitation.

Flushed with wine and apprehension the old butler stepped forward. He carried no notes, and needed none for every year the recitation was the same, the same words, the same gestures, the same inflexions. The third and final verse was the climax:

> The tempest breath sweeps o'er the sea
>   with howlings of despair,
> Death walks upon the waters, but the tar
>   must face and bear:
> The bullets hiss, the broadside pours, 'mid
>   sulphur, blood and smoke,

And prove a British crew and craft alike
   are hearts of oak.
Oh! Ye who live 'mid fruit and flowers –
   the peaceful, safe, and free –
Yield up a prayer for those who dare
   the perils of the sea.
'God and our Right!' these are the words
   e'er first upon our lips;
But next shall be, 'Old England's Flag, our
   Sailors and our Ships!'

Robinson raised his glass high and cried out with such fervour that the rafters rang:

'Ladies and gentlemen! I give you: Our sailors and our ships!'

All raised their glasses. All repeated the words. All drank. Not a few wiped away, as Robinson did, a patriotic tear. The applause was tremendous, and even Joanna was seen to smile and nod her head in approval.

But now Lady Tremaine stepped forward, clapped her hands, and called for the company to form two lines. Then like some foreign dignitary inspecting the troops Lady Tremaine walked between them, distributing gifts.

There was Turkish delight in jars, carved bears from Bavaria, and briar pipes. For Margaret there was a painted trinket box, for Robinson a gold-handled walking stick, which then and thereafter accompanied him wherever he went. Now Lady Tremaine came to an oriental table upon which were set out two special presents under damask cloths.

'Nicholas, Gerald,' she said, 'step forward.' The boys did so. 'This Christmas is a very special Christmas, for I never thought to welcome again under my roof my only grand-

son, whom for so long I believed to be lost to us for ever.'
At this there were murmurs of delight and approval, and
Nicholas stood up a little straighter and held his head up a
little higher. 'Many years ago my son, Captain Walter
Tremaine, asked Mr Penfold to carve a gift for young Sir
Nicholas, then little more than a babe in arms. Gladly he
undertook the commission, and I have here the fruits of
his labours.'

With something of a flourish she removed the cloth
from Penfold's frigate and those assembled gasped in
amazement and delight. Lady Tremaine turned to
Nicholas, and led him forward by the hand to stand right
by the ship. Then she continued: ·

'It is indeed very fine workmanship but there are those,
Nicholas, who have argued that it may be a more suitable
gift for Gerald than for you. Since it was made for you, my
darling, I believe that you should have the choice. Ah, but
what is the choice?'

She took hold of the edge of the second cloth with her
twisted fingers. Her wedding ring of diamonds and rubies
glinted brilliantly in the candlelight.

'Nicholas darling, do you recall one day when we were
down by the harbour and saw this fine coach passing by?
And although you said nothing I could see how wistfully
you stared after it as it passed. So I sent William off with
clear instructions and he returned with this.'

She nodded to Penfold. Justice had been done. And she
whipped the cover off the second present. There was a
miniature stagecoach and horses, driven by the perfect
likeness of a coachman, conducted by a most unreliable-
looking guard, and occupied by a number of fashionable
ladies and gentlemen. Again there were gasps, but these
were louder, because while Mr Penfold's frigate had been

observed and admired for some years, nobody in Trecastle had ever seen such a fine shop-bought toy as this.

'So, Nicholas darling,' Lady Tremaine concluded, 'which shall it be? Coach or ship?'

With a serious and determined air Nicholas turned to Lady Tremaine and said:

'If it please you, Grandmama, I have the ship.'

Penfold grinned hugely and there was a burst of applause from all and sundry. Only one looked displeased with the decision. Gerald stepped forward, his face scarlet with passion.

'You shan't, you young coward!' he cried. 'What good is a ship to you? I am to be the sailor and you can never be one because you are afraid of the waves. You know very well that you are!'

'Gerald!' cried Lady Tremaine sternly, 'I am ashamed of you!' But Gerald's anger was past all control.

'I tell you I will have the ship! Nicholas cares nothing for the sea. He cares only for pigs and dirty animals. He should go back to France. We don't want him here!'

'Nico, darling,' said his grandmother, 'are you quite certain in your choice?'

Nicholas turned to face the assembled company. His face was serious, and he seemed quite adult as he said:

'I do have fear of the sea. That is true. My mother she drown and my father also in the sea. But I am Sir Nicholas Tremaine and I am to be a sailor and to serve in Her Majesty's Navy and so I must love the sea. And I will. I take the ship.'

The delighted Penfold led the tumultuous applause, and the servants from the big house clustered around the baronet, cheering and shaking him by the hand. Gerald stood apart, biting his lip.

Apprehensively Joanna approached her son and cradled his head and kissed him. He pulled away. Margaret guessed what was going to happen, but too late. With a mighty sweep of his arm Gerald dashed the toys off the table. But Margaret was not the only one to have read the warning signals. Penfold stepped forward just in time to catch the frigate; but the coach and horses crashed to the floor and shattered. Gerald ran out of the room, out of the Dower House, and stood under the frosty stars, breathing deeply and muttering. Joanna came after him.

'My darling boy,' she cried. 'I'll buy you twenty ships if you want.'

'Why does he have to have everything first? Everything best? I'm twice the Tremaine he is!'

'But of course you are,' Joanna agreed, kissing him again. 'We won't mind him.' And as she cradled him to her, she whispered that he was not to give another thought to that nasty little French boy. Roughly he broke away from her and ran off into the night.

He went straight to the stables. He went straight to Peterkin. He saddled and bridled the pony and tugged him by his halter into the open air. Then he leapt on to his back and slapped him with a stick. The boy and the pony galloped off.

Chapter Twenty-Three

It was from the moment that Nico bravely chose the ship that his real troubles began.

Early on Christmas morning he made his way cheerfully to the stables. He had some sugar for Peterkin and a silver bow to tie in his mane in celebration of the season. But there was no Peterkin. Baker, the head groom, reported that when the lad from the village had arrived to muck out, he had found the pony gone and had assumed, since the tack was gone too, that Sir Nicholas had taken him off for an early morning spin. Nico was devastated. Baker suggested that they go up to the big house together and report the missing pony. There was sure to be a simple explanation, he insisted.

There was. A few miles away Gerald led the pony into a deserted cottage, where the animal stood, his foaming flanks heaving, and his nostrils flared.

'There!' cried Gerald. 'That's what it feels like to have a real rider on your back.'

In response Peterkin pawed the ground with his foot and tossed his handsome head.

'Now, you just hold still,' cried Gerald, 'while I tether you, and you'd better get used to this place, for it is to be your new home.'

It was a longish walk back to the big house, but Gerald smoothed his hair down and strolled into the breakfast room with a well-rehearsed yawn. His mother greeted him, but Margaret who could read his moods was immediately suspicious.

'Gerald,' she said, 'have you been riding Peterkin without Nico's permission?'

Gerald looked as innocent as if he had just stepped out of church.

'Why should I do that, Margaret? I do have my own pony to ride.'

At this Nicholas announced that Peterkin must have been stolen. Who could have done it, and why? Joanna found his jabbering intolerable, and said that she had a headache and was going to her room. She told Margaret to sort out her clothes because the following day she was to travel to London in time for the school term. Nicholas had heard nothing of these plans, and his wretchedness at the loss of his pony was doubled at the prospect of losing his best friend. Margaret did her best to calm him and promised she would go with him and hunt for Peterkin after lunch.

To comfort himself Nicholas took the frigate to a large rock pool high up above the high-water mark, and sailed it there for an hour or two. It looked very fine indeed with the wind in its sails. On his return to the house, Margaret, who had finished her packing, took Nico to Mr Penfold's shop, and together they wrote out a card, and gave it to

Penfold who put it in the window for them. The card told the villagers that Peterkin had gone missing, and that there would be a reward for anyone who could give information leading to his recovery.

As they left the shop Nico heard the unhappy sound of an animal in pain, and, running ahead to discover the source of the sound, reached the village water trough. There stood Joe Snell, and in his hand he had a large stone; there stood the old grey donkey, who was rather stiff in his limbs, with his leg bleeding from a recent wound; there stood Gerald watching.

Appalled, Nico ran forward shouting at Joe to stop, but he let fly with another stone, and laughed. Nico ran between the boys and the animal, and stood with his arms outstretched.

Gerald called out: 'Good! Now there are two donkeys to aim at', and Joe laughed heartily. Whereupon Nico flung himself on Joe and pulled him to the ground. Gerald would have gone to Joe's aid, but Margaret was too quick for him; Gerald found his arms pinioned, and Margaret kept tight hold.

'Let me go!' shouted Gerald.

'Indeed I will not,' Margaret replied. 'What has happened to you, Gerald?'

Gerald was not sure what had happened to him, but any confession would have lost him face with his friend, so he merely said:

'It's only an old donkey. We all know no one cares for animals like Nico!'

While this conversation was going on, Nico and Joe had been grappling on the ground. With a great heave Nico caught Joe off-balance and set him spinning into the water trough. He emerged looking like an apologetic otter. Nico

took out his handkerchief and set about binding the donkey's leg with it. Gerald found it difficult to believe that Joe had been defeated by that coward, Nico. Besides Margaret there was one other observer of the scene – Tom Austen.

That night and for several nights following, Nicholas knelt by his bedside and prayed to the porcelain Madonna, that she keep Peterkin safe and bring him back to him.

Chapter Twenty-Four

Later that day Mrs Snell paid a visit to Joanna Tremaine. She had dressed with care. A bright violet silk dress was set off with a crimson jacket and a dark blue bonnet. She tugged at the door-bell as though she intended to do it an injury. Robinson showed her into the library, but his voice was quiet as he introduced her, a sign that he was not well pleased.

'I shall summon him,' she said, 'for assault and battery and hurt feelings. Poor Joe! I fear for his health; he may be injured for life. Madam, my boy has lungs.'

'Summon whom?' asked Joanna haughtily.

'I tremble for the consequences. He has tried to murder my boy.'

'Who has?' asked Joanna. 'My son?'

'No, madam, no. That Sir Nicholas.'

This remark produced a change in Joanna. Suddenly she was all smiles.

'Sit down, Mrs Snell, rest your poor legs. It is quite a march from the village.'

'Mrs Snell plumped herself down in a chair. The colours clashed so violently with her clothes that one expected smoke to rise from the upholstery.

'Now, my dear Mrs Snell, tell me the whole story.'

Mrs Snell took a handkerchief from her handbag ready to dab her eyes.

'It was like this. My son, Joe, was playing on the green with Master Gerald. They are such pals and they play such interesting games.' And she told her story with many elaborations. The more she heard, the more Joanna liked what she heard. Her eyes shone and she leaned forward in her chair in anticipation of hearing yet more disgraceful and delightful tales about them.

Meanwhile Margaret had completed her packing upstairs, and was comforting Nicholas. She was not going to the North Pole, she told him, and he could always write to her. Besides, she felt he had become altogether too dependent on her; he must learn to fight, as he had fought that very morning with Joe Snell.

'Yes,' he bravely admitted, 'I can write and I can fight.'

It sounded so charming in his quaint French accent that Margaret could not suppress a smile. But farewells were cut short when Joanna appeared and demanded Nico's presence in the library 'on a very serious matter'.

The very serious matter turned out to be Mrs Snell's allegations, but Nicholas refused to answer these highly coloured charges. His defiance increased Joanna's anger.

'Nobody wanted you here,' she said at length. 'I rue the day that Mr Randle poked his nose in where it was not wanted. Even your grandmother never ceases to regret the day you returned to take the place of Gerald, whom she loved, and loves, as indeed we all do.'

'No, she wanted me back,' said Nicholas.

'It is not for me to punish you, but every time I look at you I shall wish that you had drowned with your mother and father. You a sailor, Sir Nicholas? Never in a hundred years!'

As she grew angrier so her voice grew louder, and Margaret thrust open the door, and cried:

'Mother, that's enough!'

'Sneaking about again, snooping and eavesdropping?'

'Mother, the whole house could hear. Do you wish to know what really happened at the water trough? I was there, Mother. Mrs Snell was not. I saw everything.'

And she proceeded to tell her mother the true version, concluding:

'As for "pneumonia", Joe Snell will suffer nothing more serious than damaged pride, which he roundly deserves, and wet clothes, which were much in need of a washing. Why do you not speak to Gerald as you have spoken to Nicholas?'

But it did no good. Joanna had no use for the truth and told Margaret not to interfere in matters which did not concern her. She expressed the hope that the Academy for Young Ladies would teach her manners and respect for her elders and betters. Then Robinson came to the door to announce that the carriage was waiting, and that if Miss Margaret did not come immediately she would miss the London train.

Nicholas ran to her and flung his arms around her. Joanna parted them. Margaret walked bravely to the carriage, while Nico climbed the stairs to his room where he sat in front of Margaret's porcelain Madonna, intending to pray, but finding no words of comfort and no love in his heart.

Meanwhile Tom Austen had called at the Dower House. In his Sunday suit and twisting his cap in his hands, he stood nervously on the doorstep until Dulcie opened the door to him.

'Whyever be you here, Tom?'

'To see 'er Ladyship.'

''Tain't her hour for receiving. She has a lie-down, see. Why, not even the Vicar would call at this time o' day, Tom.'

'But this is very pertickler business, Dulcie, an' I got meself cleaned up special.'

'I could give her a message from you, Tom. Would that meet the case?'

'It ain't message-business. I got to tell it her meself.'

'Well, you'd best come in then, but wipe your feet on the mat, and walk up gently.'

Lady Tremaine's bedroom was shuttered and curtained. The air was stifling with the scent of verbena and lavender water. The old lady lay on a couch with a rug over her legs. Tom thought of a picture he had once seen of some Roman catacombs.

'I have little love of company during the afternoons, Tom. My dreams are company enough, and the ghosts which haunt them.'

'Ghosts?' asked Tom, alarmed.

Lady Tremaine smiled a private smile. Her voice was very low and Tom had to creep closer to hear her. 'It is I they haunt. They have no business with any other.'

Tom became suddenly shy, and did not know how to tell her the news he had brought. She asked after his family, and learned that they were all well, except that little Benjamin was cutting a tooth. Lady Tremaine grew impatient.

'But you scarcely came to tell me that, Tom. Is it the Football Club subscription?'

'No, my lady, I ain't the treasury; that's Bob Croft.' Then he plucked up his courage and said in a sudden burst of eloquence: 'I came to say that Joe Snell is a coward and little Sir Nicholas is none. I wouldn't have troubled you only I seed that Mrs Snell, dressed like a parrot at the big house, and know'd that she'd 'ave gone to tell 'er tale; so I thought, Tom, tell yours, because it's the gospel truth no matter what, and I was there, my lady, and I seed what I seed.'

And he told her what he had 'seed' and concluded by remarking that Sir Nico was a born brick. 'So you see it's Joe Snell that's the coward. Not Sir Nico. Whatever the old parrot says.'

'I am grateful and proud that you told me all this, Tom, and I will ask Dulcie to give you six shillings as you leave. Two shillings you are to give Bob Croft for the Football Club, two shillings you are to give Benjamin to get something to take his mind off his bad tooth, and two shillings you are to keep for yourself.' Tom was profuse in his thanks, but Lady Tremaine said that it was she who should be thanking him. 'What you told me is worth peace of mind, Tom, and that is not something which can be bought with shillings.'

Once Tom had been shown out, his pocket jingling with unheard-of riches, Lady Tremaine sent Dulcie up to the big house with a message that she would call on her cousin in the morning on a matter of some importance.

Chapter Twenty-Five

After seeing Margaret off at the station, Gerald made his excuses and went to call on Joe. He had heard exaggerated rumours about Joe's 'pneumonia', and wished to see for himself.

His head was buzzing. He felt excited about Peterkin; it was a splendid trick to play on Nico, and one that would teach him a much-needed lesson, but he felt sorry for his cousin too. Still someone who could up-end Joe into the water trough was clearly able to look after himself. He felt sad about Margaret. They had never before been parted for more than a few hours. This time it was to be for weeks and weeks. And yet he felt proud to be, in her absence, responsible for looking after their mother.

'Joe! Joe!' he called, throwing small pebbles at Joe's bedroom window.

After a while Joe's pale face appeared.

'Joe, come down.'

'I can't. Me mam says I'm dying of a chill.'

'Come down, I say. I've got something to show you.'

There was the slamming of a door from inside the cottage.

'In the shed round the back,' hissed Joe, 'quick!' And his face disappeared.

The shed was a tidy clutter of the tools and implements of Mr Snell's profession. He was a thatcher and roof-tiler. While waiting for Joe, Gerald spotted a small cannon half-concealed among some sacking. As soon as Joe joined him he asked him about it.

'It's dad's pride and joy,' said Joe. 'He found it over Penzance way. All rusted up, it was. He's fixed it. I ain't supposed to touch it.' And he touched it. 'It's not for fighting, more for raising the alarm, Dad says.'

'Would it work?'

'Give it a good greasin', an' it might.'

''Course we'd need some powder.'

'Well, I know where we could get that.'

'You do?'

'Penfold's shop.'

The boys fell silent, as they contemplated the joys of firing off forbidden cannons. Then Gerald remembered what it was he had roused Joe for, and they set off for the deserted cottage.

There was something wrong. The door was hanging awry and blowing slightly in the rising wind.

'That's not right,' said Gerald anxiously. 'I left it shut.'

He ran ahead of Joe, and what he saw confirmed his worst fears. Peterkin was gone. The frayed end of the rope with which he had tethered him was clear evidence of what must have happened.

'Oh, this is interesting,' said Joe with heavy sarcasm. 'An

empty cottage an' a bit of old rope. This is worth getting out of me sick bed to see.'

'Be quiet, Joe, and let me think,' said Gerald.

A sudden gust of wind brought a scattering of rain and a breath of chill air from the open door.

*   *   *

Joanna had been snooping in Nico's bedroom. She had heard the window banging in a sudden gust of wind, and had entered the room in order to secure the catch; once there she found herself irresistibly tempted to investigate further.

Pride of place on the window-ledge was given to Penfold's proud frigate. Joanna was not at all pleased to be reminded of *that*. By the bed was the battered and stained copy of *Old Mother Hubbard*. There were some shells from the beach and a pencil sketch which Randle had made of him one idle afternoon. There was an apple and a bunch of fresh flowers which Margaret had picked for him before leaving for the station. And there was something under the pillow . . . She picked it up for a closer look and smiled a grim smile but, hearing the approaching footsteps of the young baronet, waited behind the door.

As Nicholas entered, Joanna pushed the door to behind him. Despite his shock at seeing her Nicholas spoke resolutely:

'Mrs Tremaine, do you want to know what happened with the donkey? What really happened? You want to know?'

Joanna held up the statue of the Madonna. 'It was under your pillow,' she said. 'What is it?'

'Our Lady,' said Nicholas.

'Yes, it is a statue of the Virgin Mary, is it not?' Nicholas agreed that it was. 'And to whom does it belong?'

'Why to Margaret.'

Joanna was triumphant. 'Hah! So you admit it!'

'*Quoi?*'

'That you stole it from Margaret. You waited until she was out of the house, and then you took it.'

'I did not steal,' cried Nicholas, outraged at the accusation. 'Indeed I did not. She borrowed it me.'

A gust of wind picked up a pile of dead leaves from the driveway and tossed them into the air. The gust died as quickly as it had come and the leaves sank slowly back.

'Borrowed! So well borrowed that I found it hidden under your pillow, safe from prying eyes. You are a coward, Nico. We all know that. You are a bully, as I recently discovered from poor Mrs Snell. And on top of that it now appears that you are a thief.'

'No,' shouted Nico, 'I am never a thief. Indeed I am not!' And he lunged at the figure which Joanna was holding in front of him tauntingly. He grabbed the Virgin's head, but Joanna was resolved not to let go. There was a sharp crack as the Madonna split in two.

At first Joanna said nothing, but walked slowly towards the door. Then she set the wrecked body of the china figure on a small bamboo table by the door. And then she spoke in a voice of ominous quietness.

'Now I understand your game, Sir Nicholas. If you can't have her, nobody will. Well, I think you had better stay in your room for the rest of the day and consider quietly and calmly why you were brought back to Trecastle, and how you are bringing disgrace to the name of Tremaine.'

She stepped out of the room and closed the door gently. But then Nicholas heard the turning of the key in the lock.

There was distant thunder in the air. Quite alone and quite without friends, and his pony gone, he lay down on the bed, buried his poor face in the pillow and wept.

Chapter Twenty-Six

When he was exhausted from weeping, Nicholas slept, but his sleep was filled with feverish dreams. His mother was drowning, and he struck out towards her across the burning water. She opened her mouth to tell him that she loved him, but out of her mouth came what at first he took to be a snake, but it was no snake, it was the tail of Peterkin.

'So that's where you've been hiding yourself,' he said. And then the tail caught fire, and his mother yelled, and was dragged under the surface. As he dived down to try to save her he felt her hair entwined around his legs, and he could not struggle free from it.

He woke to find the pillow damp under his cheek and the sheets in a tangle. The wind had strengthened from the sea, and it was a wild night. There were clatters and crashes from the park. From where he lay he could see the model of the frigate looking very real against the sea of the night, and he fancied that he could hear the whinnying of a pony. He turned the pillow over, untangled the sheets, and shut his eyes. But sleep did not come. Instead he heard again, more distinctly this time, a whinny.

Nicholas crossed to the window and peered down. It was a dark night and at first he was puzzled to see what appeared to be two stars. They were the whites of Peterkin's eyes. Nicholas felt such sudden joy that he had to cling on to the window-ledge to avoid falling.

'Peterkin,' he called gently. *'Ne t'inquiètes-toi.* Don't worry. I'm coming.'

But his door was still locked. Wrapping himself in a blanket to cover his nightshirt he returned to the window and leaned out as far as he could. His inquisitive hands touched something hard and cylindrical; a drainpipe. Carefully he swung himself out into the dark and stormy night. As his feet touched the ground, Peterkin tossed his drenched head, and snorted, and walked slowly towards him. The welcome familiar Peterkin smell was everywhere. The pony butted him gently with his head, and Nico kissed his muzzle. For a moment or two they stayed together without moving, then the boy leapt lightly on to the pony's back and they were off into the night.

An hour or so later, Ellen, the maid, who had taken Nicholas some supper, reported to Joanna that his room was empty, the window swinging open and the rain gushing in. Joanna went straight to Gerald's room.

'Have you seen him, darling?'

'Who?'

'Why, Nicholas, of course.'

'No.'

'He's gone.'

'Gone, Mama? Do you mean that he's gone for good?'

Joanna considered. 'Gone certainly,' she said, and added so quietly that Gerald was not quite sure he had heard correctly: 'At last.'

In the morning the wind had moderated, although the clouds were all in tatters as though torn to ribbons by the gales. The news of Sir Nicholas's disappearance on top of Peterkin's spread rapidly through the village. Some believed that, Joanna having made his life a misery, he had returned to Brittany. Some maintained that she had probably killed him to keep the estates for her own son, and that it was more than likely she had hidden his body in the cellars which was where bodies were usually hidden. Yet others insisted that he must have killed himself, or ridden Peterkin over the cliff in the storm, or been kidnapped for ransom. There were many more rumours than clues. In fact there were just two clues: Nicholas's open window and hoof-prints in the soft earth beneath it.

Baker searched the stables. Robinson elected to search the cellars. He had always been in charge of the wine and knew the tortuous cellars better than anybody. His old cracked voice echoed and re-echoed in those dusty catacombs as he shouted vainly for the young baronet.

Penfold and Bootle, with a crowd of villagers, beat at the hedgerows. Tom and Joe investigated the harbour, turning over nets and lobster pots, and peering into the sheds in the boat-builder's yard. Tom worked rather harder at it than Joe, who seemed little concerned about the loss of the baronet.

'We managed without him before,' he said, reasonably enough, 'an' I don't see why we shouldn't manage without him again.'

Gerald was riding Dandy towards the village when he met Lady Tremaine on her tight-lipped way to see Joanna.

Lady Tremaine had not heard of Nicholas's disappearance. When Gerald told her – not without a touch of relish – she seemed much affected. She turned pale and put a hand to her chest. Gerald wondered whether to offer her a ride up to the big house, but wisely decided against it.

'Gerald,' said the old lady, 'is it true what I have been told concerning you and Joe Snell and that poor donkey?'

Gerald looked at his feet, which was answer enough.

'I am ashamed of you. I would have expected better. How could you let Joe torment that old beast? And how could you let Nico take the blame?'

'Grandmama, I'm sorry.'

'Maybe it was being punished as a result of these false accusations that drove him away.'

'No, it wasn't. He was punished for stealing. He was locked in his room. And he deserved to be.'

'Gerald, I do not believe it. Nicholas is no thief. What is he supposed to have stolen?'

'Something of Margaret's. A china figure. Mother was furious when she found out. That's why he was locked in his room.'

Half an hour later a furious Lady Tremaine was shown into the library at the big house. To begin with she told Joanna what Tom Austen had told her about the water trough incident. She added that Gerald had admitted that that version had been the true one. He had also had the grace to apologise.

'Do you not think an apology is due from you, Mrs Tremaine, if not to me, at least to the poor child, when we find him?'

But Joanna said that she had believed Mrs Snell because she was Joe's mother, and had no apparent reason to lie. She admitted locking the boy in his room as a punishment for stealing the porcelain Madonna. And when Lady Tremaine accused her of bullying the child, she replied that Nicholas had not been her responsibility but Lady Tremaine's, and that if she, Lady Tremaine, had not been prepared to look after him, to take the trouble to get to know him, then she was in no position to criticise others.

There was some truth in this, but Lady Tremaine did not wish to recognise it. She told Joanna that it was her intention to send a telegram to Mr Apted and ask him to contact Margaret and bring her back to Trecastle. If anyone knew where Nicholas might be hiding it would be Margaret. She added that if, when Nico was found, it turned out that Joanna had been seriously maltreating him, she would not sign the settlement. Joanna and her children would have no money and no more rights in Trecastle than if they were tinkers.

The women were interrupted by Gerald's return. He said that there was no news, either of Peterkin or of Nicholas. But he and Joe had found a family of adders hibernating under a fallen tree; at least Joe had said that they were adders.

Lady Tremaine left, and no sooner had the door shut behind her than Joanna had Gerald by the shoulders and was impressing upon him the utmost importance of saying *nothing at all* to Mr Apted. If *certain allegations* could be made to stick, there might be no money at all for them, and they might have to leave Trecastle and return to London and squalor. Did Gerald understand what she was saying?

He understood rather too much.

'We were wrong to be unkind to Nico, weren't we?' he said.

Joanna did not reply directly.

'We must get to him first,' she said. 'We must make sure

he gets no opportunity to tell his tales. Now, Gerald, *think*. Where might he be?'

Chapter Twenty-Seven

Margaret might have enjoyed her time at St Luke's Academy for the Daughters of the Gentry. She might have enjoyed being released from the responsibility of looking after other people, and being looked after by others instead. She might have enjoyed learning and being away from her mother and having friends of her own age. But two things kept her from being happy.

In the first place she worried about Nicholas. She had a shrewd suspicion that Peterkin had been kidnapped by Gerald, in which case he would doubtless be returned to Nicholas in due course, because Gerald was not a vicious boy. But how would Nicholas cope in the meantime? Who would take his side?

The other thing that kept her from being happy was an incident that occurred on the first day of term. Her class had been taken to the Royal Academy, and, while most of the girls were giggling at paintings of John the Baptist or sighing in front of St Sebastian, she recognised a familiar voice in a nearby gallery. It was a room dedicated to recent portraits, and the familiar voice belonged to William Randle. She made her way to the room from which the voice was coming and there he was, handsome as ever and looking very dashing in a yellow cravat. With him was a young woman with a high-pitched voice and an irritating giggle. They were studying a picture; one of his, of course.

Margaret could not believe it; there she, Margaret, was on the imposing walls of the Academy, in a gilded frame, with people looking at her. And then she heard what William and the young woman were saying.

'A pretty little rustic, William. Where did you find her?'

'She is a Tremaine. The Cornish family of which I spoke.'

'I am jealous, my dear. Did you lose your heart to her?'

'As a matter of fact, Dolly, it was rather the other way about . . .'

Margaret rushed back to a room full of pictures of sea battles, and sank on to a bench where she felt righteous anger surging through her. She had concealed her anger with Gerald and with her mother, she had been tactful and sweet-natured and controlled for years, but she could not trust herself to confront William and be civil to him. So why not tell him truly how she felt? Whether or not he was capable of understanding her feelings of betrayal, it would do her good to say what she felt. But no sooner had she decided to create a scene than she was joined by the two girls, Daisy and Connie, who shared her room. They took her by the arm while their eyes shone with the excitement of sharing in some lively gossip.

'Who is he?'

'Go on, Margaret, tell us, do.'

'Is he your fiancé?'

'Was it him who painted your portrait?'

'Was it he, Connie, not him.'

'Yes, but was it?'

'He was ever so handsome. If it was he.'

'Not "ever so", *extremely*.'

'Well, he was, and so was she.'

'Oh go on, tell us, do.'

But Margaret wouldn't tell them, and didn't, and then in came Miss Grayson with a telegram from Trecastle and Lady Tremaine. It didn't really matter any more whether or not she would be happy at the school because the telegram said:

'Nicholas has run away. Come at once. Think where he might be. Apted will collect you. Lady Tremaine.'

*   *   *

Where was Nicholas? He was somewhere dank, dark and most uninviting. Peterkin did not care for it at all – the deserted cottage had been better than this by far – and the loose rocks under his hooves were treacherous. They were in a deserted tin mine and Nicholas was frightened, cold and hungry. Gerald had explored this place with him a couple of times and, when his mother demanded to know where Nicholas might be hiding, Gerald had told her about it and given her directions.

There was a sudden noise. Nico recoiled, and the movement caused the pony to shift and almost lose his footing. A rock was dislodged and hurtled down the old mine shaft, clattering against the walls and ricocheting from side to side until it splashed into brackish water a hundred feet or more below.

And suddenly they were not alone. Joanna was there, holding a lamp aloft. It illuminated her features, which seemed to Nicholas the features of someone with murder in her heart. She looked at him, the boy who had usurped her son, with hatred and contempt, and took a step towards him. Beneath his feet was the dread crevice, that deep funnel at the bottom of which lay death.

Chapter Twenty-Eight

'Got you!' said Joanna, taking a step towards him.
'Keep away from me,' said the boy, and held out
his frail arms. Joanna folded hers.

'So this is where you have been hiding with your precious Peterkin? Well, well, well. And you pretended that
he had been stolen so that Gerald would be blamed for that
as well. How very sly!'

'I never pretended. I did not! Peterkin *was* stolen. And
now we will both go away from this place and away from all
of you.'

As he said these words he thought maybe he could. He
imagined returning to Plougastel and telling the priest all
about it. Mère Annette and Lucie would be pleased to see
him and would understand. And Mère Annette would
cook him pancakes.

'If only you *would* go away. Nothing has been the same
since you arrived here.'

There was a silence between them and the distant thunder of waves breaking on the rocks. Peterkin fidgeted, and a small stone plummeted down the crevice.

'Why do you 'ate me?' asked Nico. 'What 'ave I done to you?'

Joanna came closer still. Nico could feel her breath on his cheek.

'Do you need to ask? You come back from the dead to steal my child's title, to take our fortune, and still you do not know why you are hated?'

The injustice of it outraged Nico. 'But I never wanted to come back. They made me. I wanted to stay in Plougastel.'

'Then why didn't you? For we never wanted you here. And now you will go and sneak your lies to your grandmother and we shall be turned out on the streets. Go back to France where you were happy. Here!' And she fumbled in her bag and produced a handful of coins which she hurled at him. 'Go! The sooner the better. Go, go!'

Too terrified to think of anything but escaping, Nicholas took hold of the frayed rope end and pulled Peterkin past the hysterical woman towards the exit from the mine. And then, once outside, he leapt on to the pony's back and galloped off across the moors, anywhere, so long as he could put distance between himself and his tormentor.

Back in the cave, Joanna sank to her knees and covered her face with her hands. What had she said? What had she done? And what had she *almost* done?

*　　*　　*

By the time Margaret and Apted returned to Trecastle, the

village was in turmoil. A constable had arrived from Truro, and more villagers had joined in the hunt, which was no longer concentrated around the big house but had extended into the surrounding countryside.

Leaning against a wall at the top of the cliff, Joe and Gerald watched all this activity with mounting concern.

'Now you're really for it,' said Joe. 'They'll find out everything.'

'It was you too,' said a chastened Gerald.

'*You* stole Peterkin.'

'What if I did? If they ask me I'll say it was you, and they'll believe me, because I live there.' He nodded in the direction of the big house. 'Then they'll send you to Australia.'

'Suppose they send you to Australia too?'

'Then I'll just pay for a passage home on the next boat. But I won't pay for one for you.'

'Why did Nico have to run off?'

'Don't ask me. We only meant it as a joke. Anyway,' said Gerald, believing what he wanted to believe, 'he'll turn up.'

'Tell you what,' said Joe. 'We've got unfinished business.'

Gerald looked puzzled. 'Have we?'

''Course we have. In Penfold's shop.'

'So we have.'

And the boys trotted off, pleased to have a distraction from the worrying activity all around them.

Chapter Twenty-Nine

Mr Apted took great pleasure in being right, and he had had a good deal of practice at it.

He flattered himself that in the Tremaine affair he had been right about Mrs Tremaine. She was a bad apple. He had hinted as much to Lady Tremaine, and now she would see that he had been right as usual. He had advised her strongly against signing any money over to Mrs Tremaine too quickly. Now she had proved to be unworthy of the charity which Lady Tremaine had been so eager to dispense. It was Apted who, on receiving Lady Tremaine's telegram about Nicholas, had taken it upon himself to inform the Cornwall constabulary. He now warned Joanna that a policeman would be coming to see her shortly to ask her questions, and that she would be well advised to stay indoors until he did.

At this very moment Margaret, still in her London school clothes, burst into the room and embraced her mother. Apted made his excuses and left.

'And now,' said Margaret, 'tell me everything that happened, Mother, everything.'

*   *   *

Outside Penfold's shop Joe and Gerald were discussing tactics.

'You're sure you know where he keeps the gunpowder?' Gerald asked.

''Course I am. I've seed it there.'

'It's probably years old. And damp. And full of mouse droppings.'

'Are you getting cold feet?'

'No, I am not.' Gerald was most indignant.

'Right then. Let's go.'

A few minutes later Joe tugged at the bell. Mr Penfold arrived at the door, red in the face and out of breath. He had been helping in the search, he explained, and had only just got back to open up the shop.

'Such terrible times we live in,' he muttered. 'No news, I suppose?'

Having established there was none, Gerald, at a nod from Joe, edged closer to the counter.

'Mr Penfold,' he said, 'I was wondering, could you tell me about any other battles you fought in?'

Delighted at being asked, old Penfold began a detailed description of the Battle of Navarino, moving the objects on the counter around to give the boy some idea of the cut and thrust of naval engagements, and embroidering the truth only a very little. But before he had completed his story, Gerald interrupted to thank him for such an interesting few minutes, and to make a dash for the door. Penfold was not best pleased, but Joe was. He had made off with a sack of gunpowder sufficient to sink a battleship and more than sufficient for a miniature cannon.

Back in the Snells' shed Joe explained how to load the cannon, and extracted from inside his shirt a length of fuse he had also taken from Penfold's shop.

'Well, it weren't doin' 'im no good,' he explained logically, 'and we couldn't 'ave done without it, now could we? So where do we go?'

They could scarcely fire off the cannon inside the Snells' outhouse and, with Trecastle thick with villagers hunting for Nico, it was hard to think of anywhere where they would be undisturbed.

'How about Puddicombe Rocks?' suggested Gerald eventually. 'We can get your old boat and sail with it round the headland. Then, even if they see us, they'll be too late to stop us.'

So it was agreed. Puddicombe Rocks it should be.

*   *   *

When Joanna had finished telling Margaret her version of the events leading up to Nicholas's disappearance, Margaret was unconvinced.

'Mother, what are you keeping from me?' she asked.

'Nothing much, my dear. There was one little scene right after you left for London. He had stolen that little china figure of yours, the one your father gave you.'

'But Mother, I gave the figure to Nico.'

There was a silence during which Margaret crossed the room to Joanna's side and took her hand. Then she added, quite kindly: 'Oh Mother, what have you done?'

'I did what I thought best,' said Joanna quietly. 'He was in the old tin mine.'

'So now you must do what I think best, Mother. You must go to Lady Tremaine, and tell her all you know. I will stay here and explain to the constable.'

At the Dower House Dulcie answered the door, and explained to Mrs Tremaine that her mistress was with Mr Apted and could not be disturbed.

'Could not or should not?' asked Joanna, and while Dulcie was trying to work this out, she added: 'Anyway she will be,' and brushed past the maid.

Lady Tremaine had been confessing her grievous faults to the solicitor, who knew all there was to know about the law, but not so much about feelings.

'He had been returned to me from the dead, my grand-son, a true Tremaine, and what did I do?'

'We cannot counterfeit our true feelings,' Apted intoned, helping himself to a second slice of cake.

'And if he is dead, there will be no third chance for me.'

'What shall you do?'

'I shall sell the estates. I shall leave Trecastle. I shall have Randle find those who truly loved my Nico, and I shall reward them. They will never know poverty as I will never know happiness again. I will engage you to deal with these matters, Mr Apted.'

Mr Apted saw months of profitable work ahead of him, and so it was with some reluctance that he asked:

'And if he is still alive?'

'Why, then I shall never speak sharply to him again, and, if he wishes it, he may come to live with me in the Dower House.'

It was at this moment that Joanna entered the sitting-room. Apted turned to her with an expression that was half guilt and half contempt.

'You have clearly misunderstood me, Mrs Tremaine,' he

said. 'My instructions were that you should wait for the policeman.'

'My business is not with you, Apted. It is with Lady Tremaine.'

Lady Tremaine took a sip of tea. 'Not now, my dear, please. I can think of nothing else but my poor, lost grandson.'

'It is of him that I wish to speak.'

'You have some fresh information? You know where he is to be found?'

Joanna took a deep breath, then bravely stated: 'I do not know where he is now. But I do know where he was last night.'

'But how can you know that?' asked Lady Tremaine, incredulously.

'Because I was with him.' And she told them of the meeting in the tin mine. 'He was there, and then he left.'

Lady Tremaine was amazed. 'And you did nothing to encourage him to come home? You did not embrace him? You did not speak to him of his warm bed and dry clothes?'

Joanna said: 'Everything was fine until William brought him back from France. If you were honest you would admit it too, and admit also that you thought Gerald a fitter heir than Nicholas.'

'Maybe I did. But if I did, knowing him and knowing you, how could I have left him in your charge, in the charge of a woman who hated him?'

'So why did you?'

'Because you are a mother. Because with Gerald and Margaret he would be a part of a family.'

'Or perhaps because children shout and play and would disturb your precious peace. And there conveniently was I. I was poor, and would be grateful to do your job for you in

155

return for a small annuity and the run of the big house.'

'Even if that is true, Mrs Tremaine, how does it excuse your being brutal to the boy?'

'I thought you would send us away,' Joanna whispered. 'I thought we would be poor again. You have never known poverty, and I could not have borne it. Not again.'

She collapsed sobbing on the sofa, and Lady Tremaine moved next to her. Gently she put her arm around the weeping woman's shoulders and comforted her. Apted cleared his throat and tactfully suggested that perhaps he should go out and inquire if there was any news of Nicholas.

Chapter Thirty

And what of Nicholas? Since his encounter with
Joanna in the tin mine, he was certain that there was
no future for him in Trecastle. They did not want him.
They wanted Gerald, a brave lad who was in love with the
sea, a rollicking, roistering sailor-boy, a true Tremaine.
And he, Nico, no longer wanted them. He had done his
best to become what they wanted him to become. He had
chosen the ship and not the coach. But still Joanna hated
him, Gerald despised him, and Lady Tremaine paid little
attention to him. Even William and Margaret had left him
to go to London. That Margaret should abandon him was
what hurt him most.

What he wanted more than anything was to return to
Brittany. And wouldn't they be pleased to see him? The
bells would ring and Mère Annette would prepare his old
bed in the corner of the room and he and Lucie would go
for long walks in the sunshine together. But how could he?
He had no wings. And as for the sea . . .

He had spent the night in one ditch and the next morning in another. He had tried so hard to find food for himself and Peterkin, but all that he came up with was a slice of bread which some traveller must have thrown from a carriage. Once he saw a train puff past and it seemed to him that Margaret's face was at a window, but he must have imagined it. Margaret was in London and would not be returning for weeks, if at all.

The wind and the rain were freshening again, and he no longer had the heart to move on. Let them find him if they wished to. He could go no further. He sat on the edge of the cliff and looked out towards his beloved Brittany. Maybe he would die there.

Down on the Puddicombe Rocks beneath him, Gerald and Joe were making the final preparations to fire the cannon. They had brought it in Joe's old boat round the headland and felt secure here. Who would come down to these rocks to look for Nico? It was a desolate spot. There were stories told in Trecastle of two boys who had gone there years before to look for a gull's nest and who had been carried out to sea, and never heard of again.

Joe had improvised a scoop to hold the gunpowder and was pouring it down the barrel.

'Is that enough?' he asked.

'It doesn't look much to me.'

Joe added another scoopful, and, taking the fuse from inside his shirt, inserted it ready for firing. They were so absorbed in what they were doing that they failed to notice how fast the tide had come in, and how high the waves were rising. Now the spray from a large wave drenched them and Joe looked up with some alarm. But Gerald was not to be diverted from the cannon, and indeed it would only be a minute or two more before they were ready to fire it.

Gerald had taken a box of matches from his pocket. At the second attempt he lit the fuse, and both the boys watched in awe as the red glow travelled ever closer to the firing pin. Then there was an almighty explosion.

In the library of the big house Robinson was tidying Joanna's desk. He heard the explosion and looked up. As Margaret walked across the park to join the searchers she heard it too, and so did Mrs Snell, as she gossiped with a neighbour. In the Dower House, as she cleared away Apted's tea-cup, Dulcie heard it and looked in alarm at Apted, who was a little deaf and did not appear to have heard anything. But Penfold, whose faculties remained razor-sharp, heard the bang and came out of his shop to see if anyone could tell him what it was. Was it the French? As Joanna and Lady Tremaine walked together in the direction of the tin mine they heard it, and so did little Sir Nicholas. Since he was so close to the source of the explosion, it sounded especially loud in his ears. He looked down the cliff, and saw Joe and Gerald on Puddicombe Rocks. He saw how the sea was swirling around them, and how Joe's boat was being carried out to sea by the current. He started to clamber down the cliff, using such hand- and footholds as he could find, and, when he could find none, slithering and slipping until he reached the shore. As he descended he shouted out to the boys, but the wind was too strong and carried his thin voice away from them.

There was another boy who heard the cannon and, from his position a little further along the cliff, spotted the boys stranded on the rocks. It was Tom Austen, who set off at once for the harbour. All the fishermen would be out, but maybe there was just one boat moored there which would take him to Puddicombe Rocks in time.

On the rocks themselves Joe and Gerald recovered from the effects of the blast and laughed at first to see each other's blackened faces and torn clothing. But then Gerald spotted the boat several yards away across open sea, and the waves running and roaring and foaming between. One of them must go for it; would Joe? He shook his head.

'It be madness, Master Gerald. Already it's too deep to wade, and if we try to swim we'll be dragged out to sea for sure.'

'Oh don't be so feeble!' cried Gerald, and stepped into the torrent. But almost at once he lost his footing and slipped, catching at a rock just in time to save himself. Joe dragged him back and Gerald emerged soaked, bruised and chastened.

'It's the spring tide,' said Joe. 'I knew as we shouldn't 'ave come.'

Gerald tried his best to be nonchalant. 'Somebody'll come soon in a boat, I suppose. They must've heard the cannon.'

'All the boats are out fishing. We're really going to fetch it, now, you see if we don't. This rock'll be under water in no time and we'll both be drowned.'

'Well, we can't be both drowned *and* punished,' said Gerald, reasonably enough.

Just then a massive wave broke right over both of them, and even Gerald uttered a wail of terror. Joe was snivelling and clinging on to the highest part of their rock with both hands, his knuckles white, his eyes tight shut, and his face contorted in terror.

Chapter Thirty-One

Behind a large rock and drawn up on the beach above the high-water mark was a battered rowing boat. Whose it was or what it was doing there was not clear. Maybe a smuggler had abandoned it; maybe a fisherman had dragged it there intending to patch it up. Whatever the reason, there was a boat, and Nicholas spotted it, and even if it was not much of a boat, it was better than nothing. He set about pulling and tugging it down towards the raging sea.

At first he could not move it. It was too heavy and he was too tired. But then, by removing the oars and by shifting it a little this way and that, he was able to release it from where it had been pinned between two rocks, then the going was easier. He slipped more than once on some seaweed and bruised his knee. The boat seemed to have a mind of its own and resisted his efforts, but eventually he reached the water's edge. Then he had to return for the two heavy, wooden oars. All the time the tide was rising higher and higher.

Finally he was ready to launch the boat, and he jumped in and started to fit the oars into the rowlocks. But try as he might the boat would not move. There was nothing for it but to jump out and push it off the shingle until it was in clear water.

The terror returned. He saw the water swirling around his knees, and he heard the wind roaring in his ears, and it was as though he was on the doomed *Alberta* once again. He pushed and he heaved and he heard the crack of the mast and the cry of the mariners. The water was above his waist, and the tide was running so powerfully that he could scarcely push the boat at all. He saw his mother's loving face, framed by her flowing hair, and heard her cry to him once more that she loved him. With a last desperate heave he lifted himself into the boat, and lay panting and exhausted inside.

Around the harbour and along the top of the cliff the villagers gathered. Tom Austen had been the first to spre the news, and now it seemed that everyone knew of the drama. Gerald and Joe were stranded on the Puddicombe Rocks and the tide was about to submerge them.

What to do? There were no boats, and by the time someone had ridden to the next harbour along the coast, it would be too late. Could somebody swim out with a line? No line would reach more than halfway to the boys, and the waves and the current meant that anyone who risked it would almost certainly fail.

'But we can't just stand here and watch them drown!' cried Mrs Snell, who was working herself up into hysterics.

'Do you have a better idea?' Apted asked her icily. He

had taken his shoes and socks off, but then quietly, when no one else was looking, he put them on again.

It was Apted who saw Nicholas first. He looked tiny as he tried to steer the rotten boat through the furious waves. It seemed impossible that a child should be able to manoeuvre such a heavy craft to where Gerald was waving his arms in desperation. By now the stranded boys were only visible from the waist up, and the white crests of waves broke all around them.

'Why, it's Sir Nicholas!' quavered Penfold, and the cry was taken up by everyone.

'Thank heaven that he's alive,' muttered Lady Tremaine fervently, casting her eyes up to heaven as she spoke. She added: 'I cannot watch,' and turned away to find herself face to face with Joanna. They grasped one another by the hand.

The boys on the rock did not see Nicholas until he was almost upon them. The waves were high and partially hid the rowing boat, which leaked profusely and was lying low in the water. When they did spot him they cheered but, just then, a wave broke right over the boat and wrenched one of the oars out of Nico's hand. How he managed to recover it he never knew.

But he reached the boys, and Gerald and Joe clambered in as best they could. Joe's teeth were chattering and his eyes staring, while Gerald was shivering uncontrollably. Joe collapsed in the bottom of the boat, but Gerald had sufficient strength to grab one of the oars from Nico and start rowing for the shore. As he did so he murmured:

'Thanks, Nico.'

It was enough.

Chapter Thirty-Two

A fishing boat making excellent speed under full sail came alongside the rowing boat shortly after the rescue. A line was thrown aboard, and Gerald caught it and held tight as the bigger boat towed the rickety smaller one to the safety of the harbour.

Great cheers rang out! But they died away when it was seen that Nicholas was slumped over, unconscious, where he sat. An improvised stretcher was quickly brought to the boat and Nicholas was most tenderly laid upon it and covered with a blanket.

'Take him to the Dower House,' Lady Tremaine commanded. 'I shall make it my personal charge to tend him and nurse him back to health and strength.'

But it was not so easy. Nicholas did not respond and no matter how often his grandmother knelt by the bed – *her* bed – in which she had installed him and no matter how gently she stroked his forehead and murmured apologies to him, he did not stir.

Sir William Wynne Williams, the distinguished London surgeon, was sent for, and instructed to spare no expense to save the boy. He was an impressive figure in his silk hat and morning suit, and said nothing until he had examined his patient. Then he announced:

'The wounds are superficial, but there are other considerations. The boy was exposed to the elements for some considerable time. He was deprived of necessary sustenance. Unless he can be brought to his senses, he will die. He will come to his senses only if he wishes to. You must do all within your power, Lady Tremaine, to nurture that desire. My account will be forwarded to you from Harley Street next Tuesday. Good day.'

'I didn't understand a word he said,' Dulcie was later to report to the under-maid, 'except the last bit, but he was *so* distinguished.'

Joe and Gerald were sitting on the jetty looking out over a sea which was now as smooth as glass. Joe had been slapped by his mother and whipped by his father. Gerald had been 'spoken to' by Margaret, which, in its way, was worse.

'It was all our fault, Joe,' said Gerald. 'All of it.'

'I knows it, Master Gerald. And he's the bravest little gent as I ever knowed, and Mother says so too.'

Tom joined them. He had come from the Dower House, where he had been sitting with Nico.

'Is there any news, Tom?' asked Gerald.

'None good. Doctor said he didn't want to live.'

'Then we must make him.'

That night while Margaret was watching by Nico's bed, Joanna entered with the model ship, which she had carried from the big house. She carefully placed it in front of the window where it could be seen from the bed.

'His breathing seems a little easier,' said Margaret, though in truth it didn't.

'He is so thin.'

And Joanna cried, natural tears of regret and affection, the most natural tears she had shed in her life. Margaret embraced her until they were joined by Lady Tremaine with steaming cups of chocolate.

'He is fading away in front of our eyes,' she said, 'like a plucked flower.'

The women drank their chocolate. The last streaks of light faded from the sky. They dozed, to be woken by a great clattering noise from downstairs, along with a heavy panting. It was a most alarming sound and they were thoroughly frightened. Margaret left the room to investigate. Gerald had Peterkin by the bridle and was leading him up the stairs. He said simply:

'I thought Nico might like to see Peterkin. In case he was worried, you see.'

With which he led the pony into the invalid's room. The pony whinnied softly. Lady Tremaine was about to demand that he be taken away at once when Nicholas opened his eyes, and in a most matter-of-fact voice said:

'Hello, Peterkin. Hello, Gerald. I am so hungry. Where is Mère Annette?'

* * *

It was a most beautiful spring day and a picnic had been laid out on the lawn. Everyone was there, that is to say all the surviving Tremaines, Tom and Peggy Austen, Apted, the Snells, old Penfold, the Reverend Clowes, Bootle and Baker, while Peterkin and Dandy were grazing a few yards away. The servants were in attendance under the supervision of Robinson, with Dulcie waiting on Lady Tremaine.

Little Sir Nicholas was the centre of attention as it was his birthday, but he had a faraway look in his blue eyes. Suddenly several carriages came rattling up the driveway.

'I promised you a surprise, Nicholas,' said Lady Tremaine with a twinkle, 'and this, I believe, is it.'

The carriages drew up in front of the big house and from them poured a happy collection of visitors, including Mère Annette, Lucie, and a fair proportion of the population of Plougastel. At first Nicholas could not believe his eyes, but then, when he saw how Mère Annette and Lucie clearly recognised him, he opened his arms and ran to them, embracing first one and then the other as the tears ran down his cheeks.

There was an almighty flash and there was William Randle behind a vast contraption: the latest thing from London, a camera.

Epilogue

Many years have passed. We find ourselves in the studio of a fashionable photographer, William Randle. He has on his easel a mounted and framed photograph depicting a picnic in front of a grand house in Cornwall.

Randle is holding forth to a small group of visitors.

'My first successful venture into the field of photography,' he is saying. 'An idyllic scene, you will agree.'

And then over toasted tea-cakes, he tells them the whole story of Little Sir Nicholas. They wanted to know what had heppened to all the people in the story, and William told them.

'Peterkin grew to be extremely old, extremely plump, and more than a little quarrelsome. Dandy, I fear, ate too many carrots one day and died an hour afterwards.

'Joe Snell became the village carpenter and married Peggy Austen, Tom's sister. They named their first and only son Nicholas. Tom became the village schoolmaster, but could never keep order, and never married, though he had several offers.

'As for Gerald and Nicholas, both became sub-lieutenants in the Royal Navy, serving on the good ship *Trojan* at the Battle of Alexandria. Gerald was injured in that bitter conflict, and earned himself a medal, for he threw himself in front of his cousin and saved his life. He lives at the big house, where he is Sir Nicholas's steward and estate manager, for the Baronet has little time for such things now that he has been made Admiral of the Fleet. Nicholas married Lucie from Brittany and they have two daughters and a son. The son, Walter, is a midshipman and has the true Tremaine sparkle in his bright blue eyes.

'Lady Tremaine died in her sleep a year after this photograph was taken and a week before Robinson, her loyal retainer. Joanna Tremaine has, I hear, entirely abandoned her grand ways and has moved far away. She has a family of waifs and strays, whom she either spoils or bullies depending upon her mood. Mère Annette? Goodness knows. But I do know that after Penfold died, Old Nolan was pleased to be invited down to run the village shop, which he did with considerable charm and eccentricity for many years.

'As for Margaret, she grew into a beautiful young woman and eventually did me the honour of becoming my wife. We still visit Trecastle occasionally, but it is much changed. Our children love to play around the rusted cannon, and never tire of hearing my wife repeat the story of how Azicklezad rescued his friends from the raging seas and how Peterkin rescued him.

'Now, would anyone care for a cup of tea?'